Adobe® Illustrator®
for the Mac
fast&easy™

Check the Web for Updates

To check for updates or corrections relevant to this book and/or CD-ROM visit our updates on the Web at http://www.prima-tech.com/support/.

Send Us Your Comments:

To comment on this book or any other PRIMA TECH title, visit our reader response page on the Web at http://www.prima-tech.com/books/book/comment.

How to Order

For information on quantity discounts, contact the publisher: Prima Publishing, P.O. Box 1260BK, Rocklin, CA 95677-1260; 916-787-7000. On your letterhead, include information concerning the intended use of the books and the number of books you want to purchase. For individual orders, turn to the back of this book for more information.

Adobe® Illustrator®
for the Mac
fast&easy™

C. Michael Woodward
Bruce Swan

A DIVISION OF PRIMA PUBLISHING

A Division of Prima Publishing

Prima Publishing and colophon are registered trademarks of Prima Communications, Inc. PRIMA TECH and fast & easy are trademarks of Prima Communications, Inc., Roseville, California 95661.

Publisher: Stacy L. Hiquet
Associate Marketing Manager: Heather Buzzingham
Managing Editor: Sandy Doell
Acquisitions Editor: Kevin Harreld
Project Editor: Estelle Manticas
Technical Reviewer: David Fields
Copy Editor: Fran Blauw
Interior Layout: William Hartman
Cover Design: Prima Design Team
Indexer: Katherine Stimson

Adobe, Illustrator, and Photoshop are trademarks or registered trademarks of Adobe Systems Incorporated in the U.S. or other countries.

Important: Prima Publishing cannot provide software support. Please contact the appropriate software manufacturer's technical support line or Web site for assistance.

Prima Publishing and the author have attempted throughout this book to distinguish proprietary trademarks from descriptive terms by following the capitalization style used by the manufacturer.

Information contained in this book has been obtained by Prima Publishing from sources believed to be reliable. However, because of the possibility of human or mechanical error by our sources, Prima Publishing, or others, the Publisher does not guarantee the accuracy, adequacy, or completeness of any information and is not responsible for any errors or omissions or the results obtained from use of such information. Readers should be particularly aware of the fact that the Internet is an everchanging entity. Some facts may have changed since this book went to press.

ISBN: 0-7615-3502-0

Library of Congress Catalog Card Number: 00-139770

Printed in the United States of America

00 01 02 03 04 DD 10 9 8 7 6 5 4 3 2 1

For Connie and John—hanging in there since 1950.
Now that's inspiration.

Bruce Swan

Acknowledgments

As this is my first shot at writing a computer book, I'd like to thank the people at Prima Tech for the opportunity, and for their patience and help. Thanks to Tech Editor David Fields for his diligence in making sure everything works like I said it does; copy editor Fran Blauw for minding all of my P's and Q's and all the punctuation in between; and especially to Estelle Manticas, the poor sucker who got stuck with this book. It's much better thanks to her professionalism and sticktuitiveness. A tip of the hat to Lisa Bucki, author of *Photoshop 6 for Mac fast & easy*, for clearing the path and giving me some ideas on how to approach this beast. Many thanks to my sister Lori, the other published Swan, for throwing my name in the hat and for all of her help, glossary and hang-in-there-wise. Thank you Andi, Stephi, and Payton Swan for letting Uncle Bruce use their class pictures (how does it feel to be famous now?), and of course to my co-author, Michael Woodward, for wrangling all the strays and keeping the sky from falling.

About the Authors

Bruce Swan has been using Macintosh computers for graphic design since 1989, and has had one loaded with Adobe Illustrator and all of its progressive upgrades since 1991. His foray into computer book publishing began in 2000 as Technical Editor for Photoshop 6 for Mac fast & easy, also from Prima Tech Publishing. Bruce has won numerous awards for logo and event-identity graphics and design. Adobe Illustrator for the Mac Fast & Easy is his first book.

C. Michael Woodward recently moved to Tucson, Arizona after spending the first 37 years of his life in Indianapolis. He is a Senior Technical Writer for Analysts International, Inc., and is the founder of Echelon Editorial and Publishing Services, which provides freelance writing, editing, and project management services to the technical publishing industry. Michael has authored or contributed to more than a dozen computer books, including *Microsoft Outlook 2002 fast & easy*, *Create FrontPage 2002 Web Pages in a Weekend*, *Microsoft Windows 2000 fast & easy*, *Microsoft Outlook 2000 fast & easy*, *Create FrontPage 2000 Web Pages in a Weekend*, *Microsoft Money 99 fast & easy*, and many others. He's currently spending all his free time exploring his new home state, which is a full-time job in itself.

Contents

PART II
MAKING SOME ART. 35

Introduction

This *Fast & Easy* guide from Prima Tech will send you on the road to success with Adobe Illustrator 9 for the Macintosh, whether you are an absolute beginner with art and drawing programs or simply new to Illustrator 9. Illustrator 9 is packed with scores of remarkable features—in fact, it is arguably the most robust application of its kind. With the help of this book, you'll learn to take full advantage of the whole package and be well on your way to becoming a digital artist.

Adobe Illustrator for the Mac Fast & Easy teaches techniques that will enable you to create amazing illustrations and drawings of any kind, from business logos to Web page graphics, and more. You also will learn how to use filters, transformers, and other tools on images that you've created from scratch, scanned, or shot from a digital camera.

If you want to create high-quality artwork and have the widest variety of tools and controls, Illustrator 9 and this book provide everything you need to spark your creative drive and build effective, extraordinary works of art.

Who Should Read This Book?

This book is geared toward readers who are new to vector drawing packages or to Illustrator. Because it's so rich with features, Illustrator can be tough to learn. Because nearly every step in this book includes a clear illustration, however, you won't have to struggle to learn a procedure or find the right tool in the toolbox. The easy-to-understand, nontechnical language also helps smooth the transition from newbie to comfortable user.

With each task clearly identified by a heading, you'll find it easy to use the table of contents to find the steps you need. So, whether you want to work through the book from beginning to end or find just the tricks you need, this book will accommodate your style and enhance your results.

Added Advice to Make You a Pro

Once you get started, you'll notice that this book presents many steps, with little explanatory text to slow you down. Where warranted, however, the book presents these special boxes to highlight key issues:

- **Tips** give you shortcuts or hints about the ins and outs of Illustrator 9 for the Macintosh.

- **Notes** offer more detailed information on a feature, food for thought, or guidance to help you avoid problems or pitfalls in your work.

In addition to valuable appendixes at the end of the book, you'll find a glossary that explains key terms that you need to understand to work effectively in Illustrator.

Whether you're starting from scratch or have an illustration you want to edit, have fun as you dive in now!

PART I

Getting Acquainted with Illustrator

NOTE

Sometimes a command or screen item will appear "grayed out" and cannot be selected. If so, it means the command is not currently available. You may need to perform another action before you can use the command. For example, before you can use the Cut command, you must select an object in your drawing.

Following are the dialog box controls you'll run across while working in Illustrator, and how to use each:

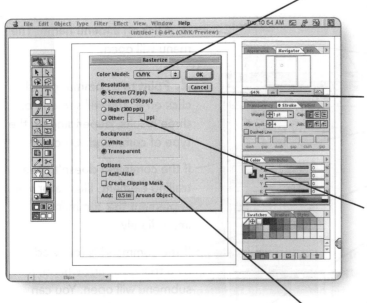

Pop-up menu. Click on a box with a double-headed arrow and a pop-up menu will open. Move the pointer through the menu and click to select an option.

Option button. Click on an option button to select it. Any other option buttons in the group will automatically be deselected.

Text box. Point to a text box, click, then just start typing. If the box already contains text, click and hold the mouse button while you drag over a text box to select it, and then type in a different entry.

Check box. Click on a check box to check or clear (uncheck) it.

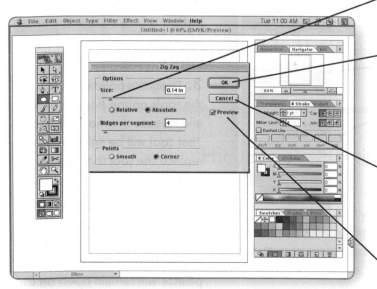

Slider. Drag the slider to increase or decrease a setting.

OK button. Click on OK to execute the command after all the adjustments are made. The command will be applied and the dialog box will close.

Cancel button. Click on Cancel to abort the procedure. The dialog box will close and no changes will be made.

Preview check box. Check this box to see a preview of an action or effect before you complete the command.

Toolbox and Palettes

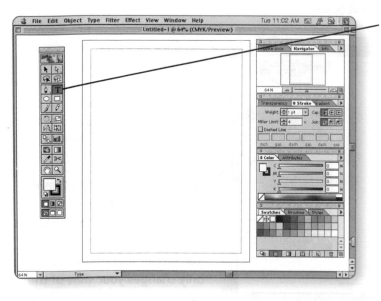

1. Click on a **tool** in the toolbox. The tool area box will be highlighted, and the tool will become active. When you move the cursor over the work area, the cursor will change to a facsimile of that tool.

Creating a New File

Illustrator lets you create a canvas as large or small as you need to fit the work you plan to do. When you create a new file, Illustrator also asks you to specify the size of your artboard and select a color mode.

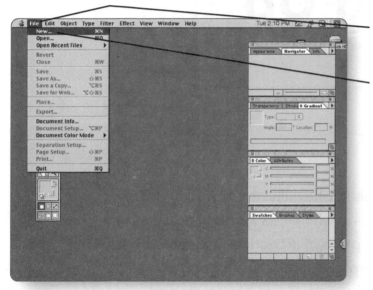

1. Click on **File**. The File menu will open.

2. Click on **New**. The New Document dialog box will appear and a temporary file name will be highlighted.

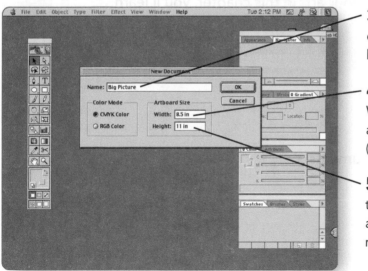

3. Type a **name** for your document in the Name text box.

4. Click and drag inside the Width box to select it, and **type** a new **width measurement** (if needed).

5. Click and drag inside the Height box to select it, and **type** a new **height** measurement (if needed).

TIP

If you don't indicate otherwise, Illustrator will use the default units of measure (usually inches). If you type another unit (such as 800px or 15cm), Illustrator will automatically convert what you type to the default units.

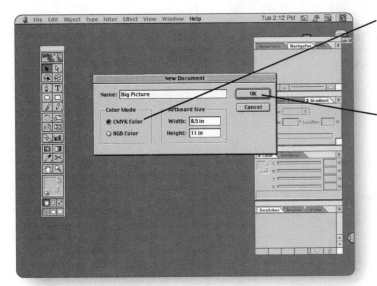

6. Click on either the **CMYK Color** or **RGB Color** option button. The desired color mode will be selected.

7. Click on **OK**. The New Document dialog box will close and a new image document file will appear on the monitor.

Opening a Saved Image File

If you have a work in progress or another saved image that you'd like to see, you can open it at any time. You can have more than one document open at the same time.

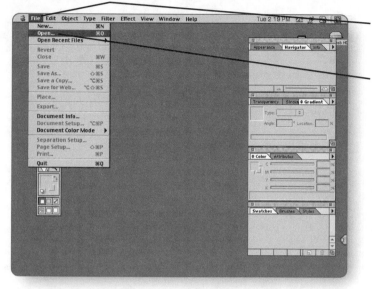

1. Click on **File**. The File menu will open.

2. Click on **Open**. The Open dialog box will appear.

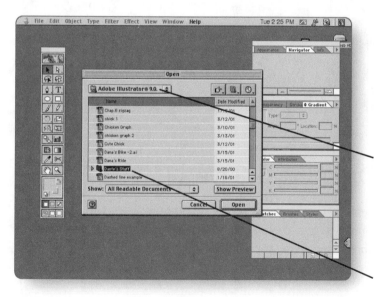

3. Locate the **file** you want on your computer. Depending on where the file was stored, you may have to do a little exploring before the file name appears in the Name list.

* Click on the Location pop-up menu. When the menu opens, click on the icon for the disk that holds the file.

OR

* Double-click on the folder icons in the list to open the folder that holds the file you want.

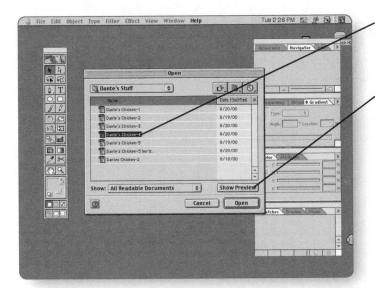

4. Click on the **file** that you want to open. The file name will be highlighted.

5. Click on the **Show Preview button**. A thumbnail of the selected file will appear.

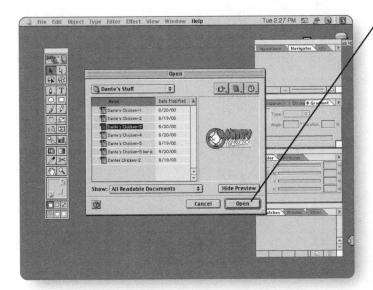

6. Click on **Open**. The selected file will open.

TIP

If you want to open a file that you have worked on recently, click on the File menu and drag the pointer down to the Open Recent command. Then click on the desired file in the submenu that appears.

Saving a File in Illustrator

It's always a good idea to save and name a newly-created or placed file to your system's hard drive. There's nothing quite like spending hours on a masterpiece, only to have it evaporated by a power outage or an errant cat pouncing on the surge protector switch.

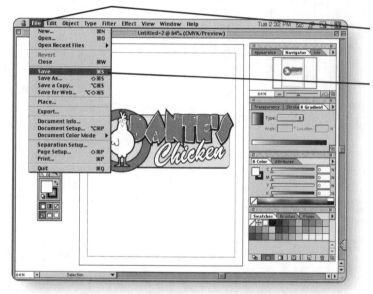

1. Click on **File**. The File menu will open.

2. Click on **Save**. The Save dialog box will appear.

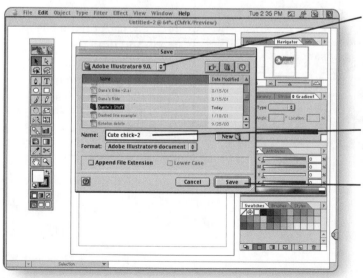

3. Click on the **pop-up menu** at the top of the dialog box, and **navigate** to the **folder** in which you want to save the document.

4. Replace the **file name** in the Name text box (if needed).

5. Click on **Save**. The Save dialog box will close and Illustrator will leave the file open for you to continue your work.

Saving Your File in a Different Format

Illustrator will save files to the Adobe Illustrator Document format by default. If for some reason you need to save your file as an Illustrator EPS or Adobe PDF file, you can do that from the Save document box.

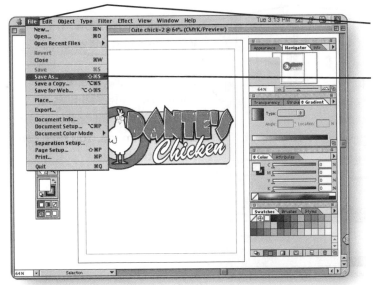

1. **Click** on **File**. The File menu will open.

2. **Click** on **Save As**. The Save dialog box will appear.

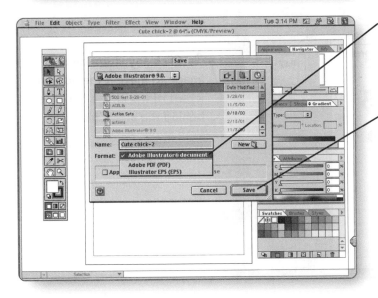

3. **Click** on the **Format pop-up menu** and **select** the correct **format** (usually the default setting is fine).

4. **Click** on **Save**. Illustrator will change the format and the Save dialog box will close.

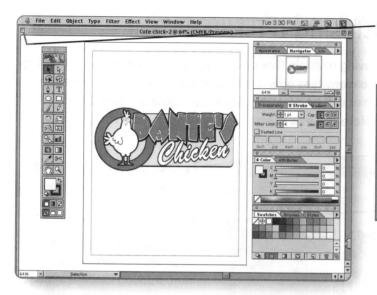

4. Click on the **Close button**. The document will close.

Part I Review Questions

1. How do you open a new Palette? *See "The Toolbox and Palettes" in Chapter 1*

2. If a command on a menu is followed by an ellipsis, what will happen if you click on it? *See "The Menus, Submenus, and Dialog Boxes" in Chapter 1*

3. What does it mean when a command is "grayed out?" *See "The Menus, Submenus, and Dialog Boxes" in Chapter 1*

4. How do you zoom in on the artboard? *See "Toolbox and Palettes" in Chapter 1*

5. How do you hide a toolbar when you're not using it? *See "Hiding and Showing the Toolbox and Palettes" in Chapter 1*

6. What kind of help with using Illustrator 9 does Adobe offer? *See "Getting Help" in Chapter 1*

7. How do you specify the size of your artboard when opening a new file in Illustrator? *See "Creating a New File" in Chapter 2*

8. How do you quickly save you work in progress? *See "Saving a File in Illustrator" in Chapter 2*

9. If you wanted to save your document as a PDF, where would you specify that information? *See "Saving Your File in a Different Format" in Chapter 2*

10. How do you switch between two open documents? *See "Switching between Open Documents" in Chapter 2*

PART II

Making Some Art

3

Drawing Tools

So there you sit with a million wonderful ideas in your head and a blank digital sheet of paper on your screen. Oh, the possibilities! Illustrator has all the tools you need to communicate those ideas to the world. As you saw in Chapter 1, the toolbox contains everything you will use to create and manipulate your images. Illustrator offers two categories of tools: drawing and painting. Let's focus first on the drawing tools. In this chapter, you'll learn how to …

- Explore the Ellipse, Rectangle, and other preset shape tools
- Use the Pen tool
- Use the Pencil tool

Using the Preset Shape Tools

Drawing and manipulating shapes (or objects) is the basis for creating any image in Illustrator. In the toolbox, you will find several preset shape tools that automate the task of drawing simple closed geometric shapes, such as ellipses, rectangles, polygons, stars, and spirals.

Drawing an Ellipse

Follow these steps to draw a simple ellipse:

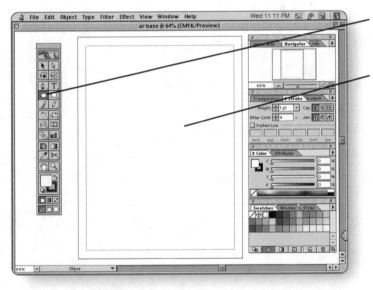

1. Click on the **Ellipse tool**. The tool will become active.

2. Click on the **artboard** where you want to place the object and **drag diagonally**. A wireframed outline of the object will appear.

TIP

To draw a preset shape from its center outward, press and hold the Option key while dragging.

To draw a perfect circle with the Ellipse tool, or a perfect square with the Rectangle tool, press and hold the Shift key while dragging.

To move a shape while you're drawing it, press and hold the spacebar.

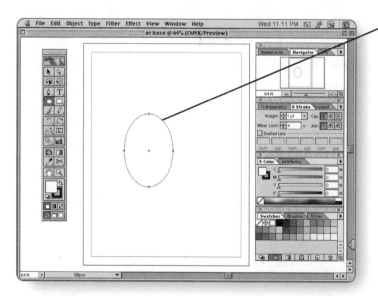

3. **Release** the **mouse button** when the ellipse is the size and shape you want. The finished object will appear onscreen.

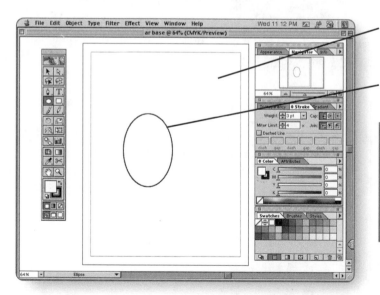

4. **Command+click** on a **blank area** of the artboard.

The object will be deselected.

TIP

To delete an object, click on it with the Selection tool to select it (if needed) and press Delete.

Drawing a Rectangle

The steps to create a rectangle are nearly identical to those for ellipses:

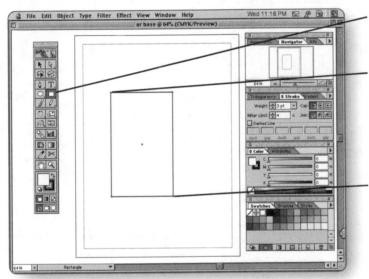

1. **Click** on the **Rectangle tool.** The tool will become active.

2. **Click** on the **artboard** where you want to place the object and **drag diagonally.** A wireframed outline of the object will appear.

3. **Release** the **mouse button** when the rectangle is the desired size and shape. The finished object will appear onscreen.

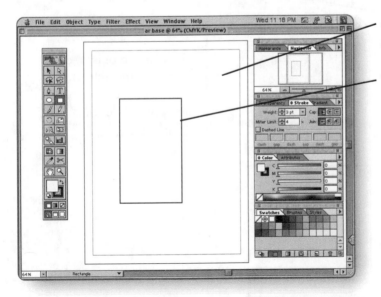

4. **Command+click** on a **blank area** of the artboard.

The object will be deselected.

Drawing a Shape with Specific Dimensions

Sometimes you need more precision than you can get by drawing with the mouse. When that's the case, you can customize a rectangle or ellipse by entering its exact width and height. In this example, we'll draw a rectangle; the steps for the Ellipse tool are the same.

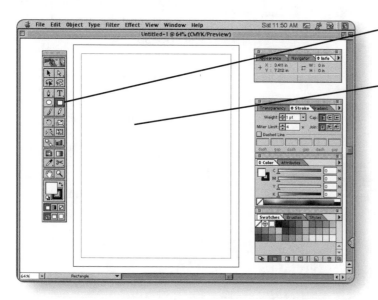

1. Click on **Rectangle tool**. The tool will become active.

2. Click on the **artboard** where you want to place the upper left corner point of the object. (Don't drag, just click.) The Rectangle dialog box will appear.

TIP

Hold down the Option key when you click the location to place the center point of the rectangle instead of the corner point.

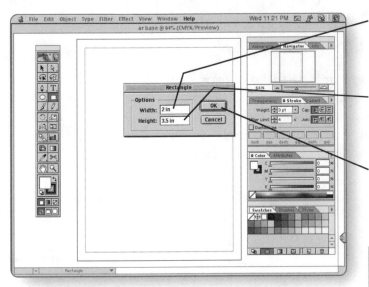

3. Click and drag inside the Width text box to select it, and enter a value.

4. Click and drag inside the Height text box and enter a value.

5. Click on OK. The dialog box will close, and the wireframe will appear.

TIP
You can press the Tab key to move between dialog box items to select them sequentially.

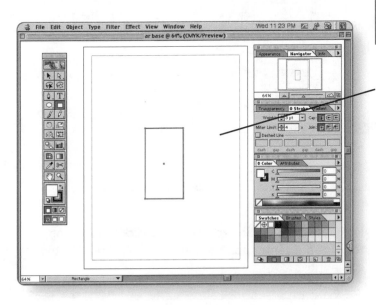

6. Command+click on a blank area of the artboard. The object will be deselected.

Drawing Special Shapes

In addition to the basic rectangle and ellipse, Illustrator's toolbox includes a variety of more complex preset shapes to save you time and effort. In this section, you'll learn to create polygons, stars, spirals, and rounded rectangles. You'll find these shortcut shapes tucked away in the Ellipse and Rectangle tool pop-out palettes.

Drawing a Polygon

A polygon is an object that consists of at least three straight line segments; each line segment joins two others at their end points, and the segments form a completely closed outline. Triangles, squares, pentagons, and octagons are all examples of polygons.

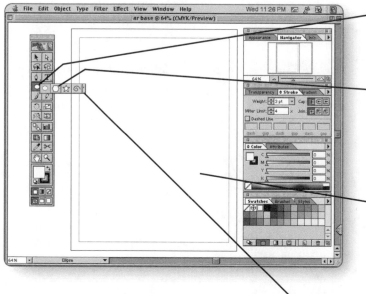

1. **Click and hold** the **mouse button** over the Ellipse tool. A pop-up palette will appear.

2. **Point** to the **Polygon tool** and **release** the **mouse button**. The Polygon tool will become active and will replace the Ellipse tool in the toolbox.

3. **Click** on the **artboard** where you want to place the center point of the polygon. The Polygon dialog box will appear.

TIP

For easy access to all of the tools, you can "tear off" any tool set into a floating palette. Drag the open pop-up palette away from the toolbox by dragging the pointer all the way to the right of the palette and selecting the tear-off bar with the little arrowhead.

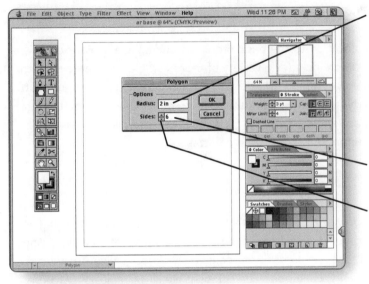

4. Click and drag inside the Radius text box and enter the radius value.

5. Enter the desired number of sides in either of the following ways:

- Double-click in the Sides text box and enter a value.

- Click on the Sides up or down arrow to increase or decrease the value.

6. Click on OK. The Polygon dialog box closes, and the wireframe will appear.

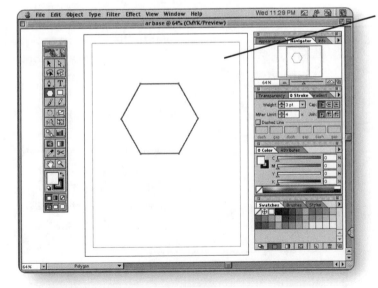

7. Command+click on a blank area of the artboard. The object will be deselected.

A *Star Is Born!*

In the early days of drawing programs, creating a star required several complex steps, but why go to all that trouble now? Adobe knows this is a popular shape, so it added a Star tool right in the toolbox. How convenient!

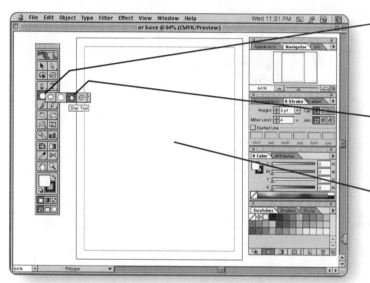

1. **Click and hold** on the **Ellipse** or **Polygon tool** (whichever is showing). A pop-up palette will appear.

2. **Point** to the **Star tool** and **release** the **mouse button**. The tool will become active.

3. **Click** on the **artboard** where you want to place the center point of the star. The Star dialog box will appear.

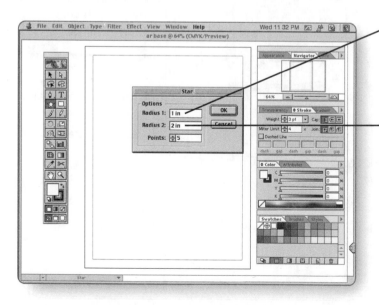

4. **Click and drag** in the **Radius 1 text box** and **enter** the **radius value** for the inner points of the star.

5. **Click and drag** in the **Radius 2 text box** and enter the **radius value** for the outer points of the star.

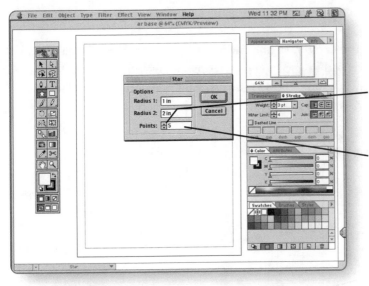

6. Enter the desired **number of sides** for the star in one of the following ways:

- **Click** on the **Points up** or **down arrow** to increase or decrease the value.

- **Double-click** in the **Points text box** and enter a value.

7. **Click** on **OK**. The Star dialog box will close, and the wireframe will appear.

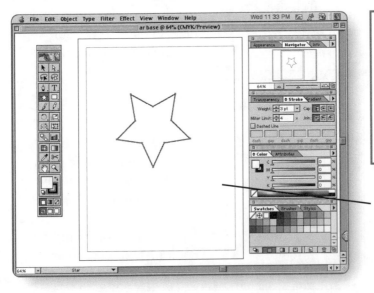

TIP

The difference between the two radius values will determine the width of the arms on your star. The shorter the difference, the wider the arms will be.

8. **Command+click** on a **blank area** of the artboard. The object will be deselected.

Drawing a Spiral

You never know when you might need to draw a whirlpool, a snail, or a watch spring. This section shows you how to do those things in nothing flat.

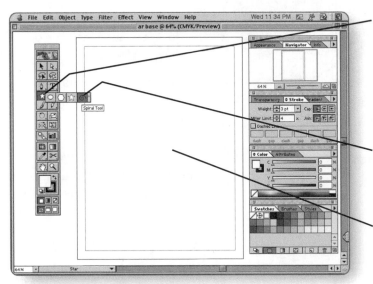

1. **Click and hold** on the **Ellipse tool** or whatever tool is occupying the Ellipse tool box. (If you've just used the Star tool, it will be visible.) A pop-up palette will appear.

2. **Point** to the **Spiral tool** and **release** the **mouse button**. The tool will become active.

3. **Click** on the **artboard** where you want to place the center point of the spiral. The Spiral dialog box will appear.

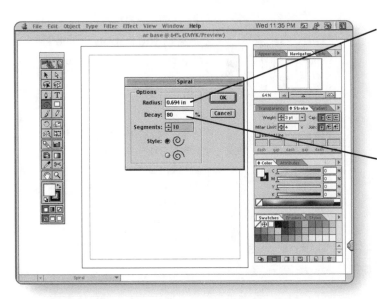

4. **Click and drag** in the **Radius text box** and **enter** a **value**. This value will represent the distance from the center to the outermost point of the spiral.

5. **Click and drag** in the **Decay text box** and **enter** a **value** between 5 and 150. This value will determine the tightness or intensity of the spiral.

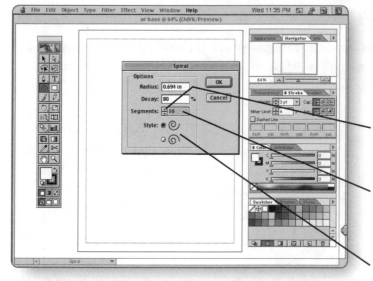

6. **Enter** the desired **number of segments** (quarter revolutions around the center point) for the spiral in one of the following ways:

- Click on the Segments up or down arrow to increase or decrease the value.

- Click and drag in the Segments text box and enter a value.

7. **Click** on the **clockwise** or **counterclockwise Style button** to determine the direction of your spiral.

8. **Click** on **OK**. The Spiral dialog box will close, and the wireframe will appear.

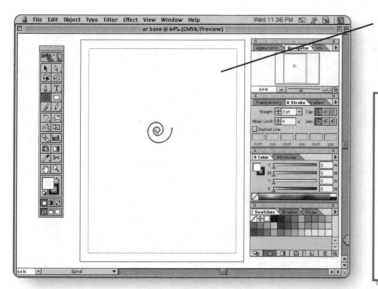

9. **Command+click** on a **blank area** of the artboard. The object will be deselected.

TIP

Rather than enter precise dimensions, you can draw a polygon, star, or spiral on-the-fly using the click-and-drag method described for the Ellipse and Rectangle tools earlier.

Drawing a Rounded Rectangle

What if you want a normal-shaped rectangle, but you want to round off the corners—like a TV screen or airplane window? No problem: meet the Rounded Rectangle tool.

TIP

As with the previous shapes, you can draw a rounded rectangle with the click-and-drag method instead of using the following steps.

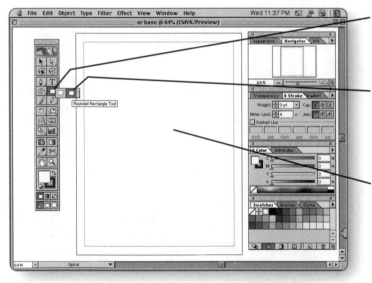

1. **Click and hold** on the **Rectangle tool**. A pop-up palette will appear.

2. **Point** to the **Rounded Rectangle tool** and **release** the **mouse button**. The tool will become active.

3. **Click** on the **artboard** where you want to place the upper left corner of your rounded rectangle. The Rounded Rectangle dialog box will appear.

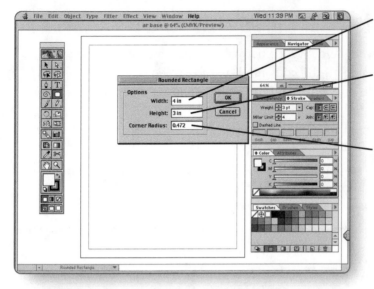

4. Click and drag in the **Width text box** and **enter** a **value**.

5. Click and drag in the **Height text box** and **enter** a **value**.

6. Click and drag in the **Corner Radius text box** and **enter** a **value**.

7. Click on **OK**. The dialog box will close, and the wireframe will appear.

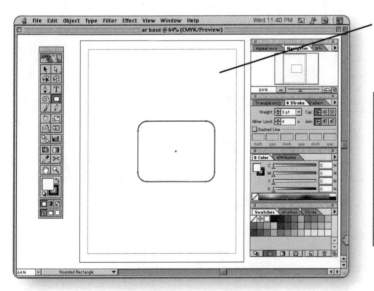

8. Command+click on a **blank area** of the artboard. The object will be deselected.

TIP

Press the up and down arrow keys on the keyboard while you hold down the mouse button to edit the curve of the corners.

Drawing Freeform Objects

You certainly don't have to restrict your drawing to geometric or closed shapes. Sometimes you need an open-ended line or a shape that's less symmetrical. The Pencil and Pen tools allow you to get wild and free with your drawing. Let's look at the Pencil tool first.

Using the Pencil Tool

Before you begin drawing with the Pencil tool, you'll want to set up characteristics for the object you're about to create. Otherwise, you might not get the results you expected.

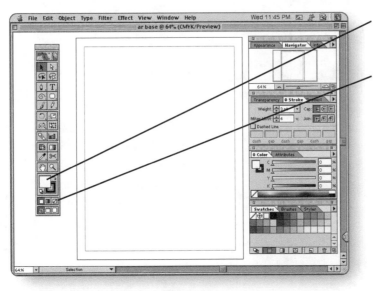

1. **Click** on the **Fill box**. The box will become active.

2. **Click** the **None button**. No fill will be applied to the Pencil-drawn object.

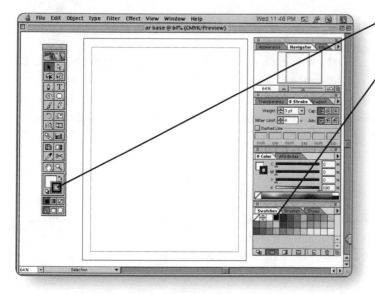

3. **Click** on the **Stroke box**. The box will become active.

4. **Click** on a **color** in the Swatches palette. The color you choose will be the color of the line you draw.

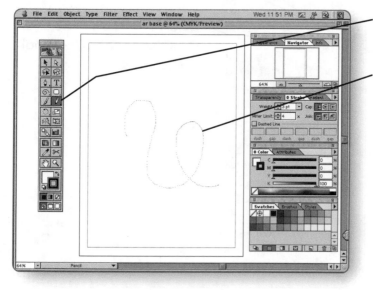

5. **Click** on the **Pencil tool**. It will become active.

6. **Click** on the **artboard, hold down** the **mouse button**, and then **drag** the **pointer** around the screen. A dotted line will appear indicating your path.

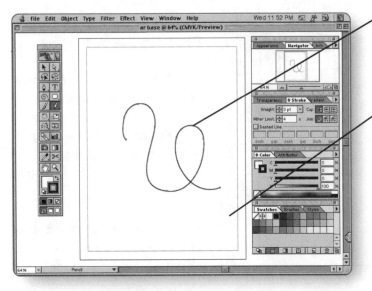

7. **Release** the **mouse button**. A pencil line will replace the dotted line, and the object's anchor points will appear.

8. **Command+click** on a **blank area** of the artboard. The object will be deselected.

Using the Pen Tool

The Pen tool is, in my opinion, the real meat and potatoes of Adobe Illustrator. It draws free-form objects like the Pencil tool, but it also draws straight lines and very precise curves.

Drawing a Straight Line

For everyone who claims that they can't even draw a straight line: no more excuses!

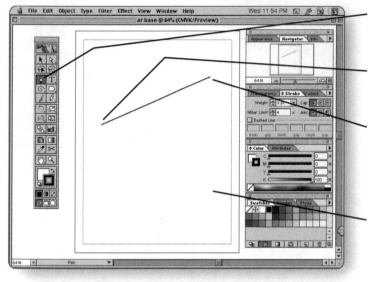

1. Click on the **Pen tool**. The Pen tool will become active.

2. Click on the **artboard** where you want to start the line.

3. Click on the line's **ending point**. The selected line will appear with an anchor point at each end.

4. Command+click on a **blank area** of the artboard. The object will be deselected.

Drawing a Zigzag Line

Try this method when you need to draw shark teeth or a range of Alps. Pinking shears, eat your heart out.

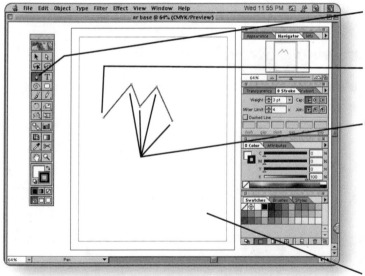

1. Click on the **Pen tool**. The Pen tool will become active.

2. Click on the **artboard** where you want to start the line.

3. Click on the next **zig or zag point**. The selected line segment will appear with an anchor point at each end. Repeat this step until you have a zigzag line with five anchor points as shown in the figure.

4. Command+click on a **blank area** of the artboard. The object will be deselected.

Drawing a Closed Object

When you stop drawing at the same place you started you will create a closed object.

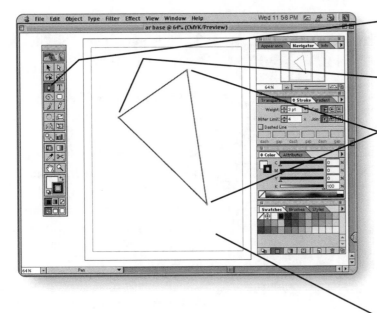

1. Click on the **Pen tool**. The tool will become active.

2. Click on the **artboard** where you want to start the line.

3. Move the **pointer** and **click again** for each desired point in the object.

4. Click on the **first anchor point** again. The paths join into a closed triangle with three anchor points, and the resulting wireframe will be selected.

5. Command+click on a **blank area** of the artboard. The object will be deselected.

NOTE

When you pass the pointer over the original starting point, a small circle will appear near the pointer. To make sure the object is closed, click when the circle is visible.

Drawing an Arc

If you're working on a brochure about a McDonald's restaurant in St. Louis, Missouri, you'll be using this tool extensively.

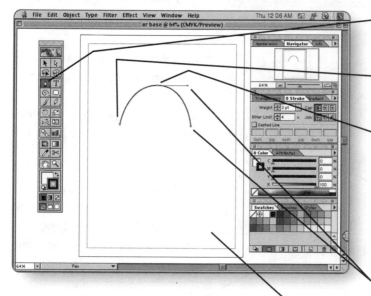

1. **Click** on the **Pen tool**. The tool becomes active.

2. **Click** on the **artboard** where you want to start the arc.

3. **Click and hold down** the **mouse button** while dragging horizontally to the right until the first half of the arc is correct and release the mouse button. The left side of the arc will appear.

4. **Move** the **pointer** down and to the right and **click once**. The remaining half of the selected arc will appear.

5. **Command+click** on a **blank area** of the artboard. The object will be deselected.

Drawing a Wavy Line

A wavy line can be created much like the zigzag line, except you will click and drag on your zig and zag.

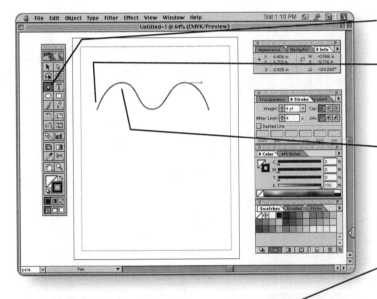

1. **Click** on the **Pen tool**. The Pen tool becomes active.

2. **Click** on the **artboard** where you want to start the line. The initial anchor point for the line appears.

3. **Move** the **pointer** up and to the right, **click and drag** horizontally to the right, then **release** the **mouse button**. A new curved segment of the line appears.

4. **Move** the **pointer** down and to the right, **click and drag** horizontally right again, then **release** the **mouse button**. A new curved section will appear.

5. **Move** the **pointer** up and to the right again, **click and drag** horizontally to the right, and **release** the **mouse button**. Another curved section will appear.

6. **Move** the **pointer** down and to the right and **click again**. A selected wavy line appears with five anchor points.

7. **Command+click** on a **blank area** of the artboard. The object is deselected.

Drawing a Closed Object with Both Points and Curves

OK now let's put it all together and draw something we can recognize.

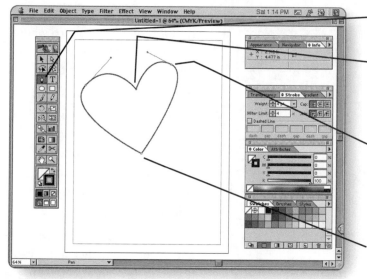

1. **Click** on the **Pen tool**. The tool becomes active.

2. **Click** on the **artboard** where you want to start the object. The initial anchor point for the line appears.

3. **Move** the **pointer** up and to the right of the first anchor, and **click and drag** to the **right and down**. Release the mouse button.

4. **Click once** on a place somewhere below the first anchor. A curved section will be created.

5. **Move** the **pointer** up and to the left of the first anchor point and **click and drag up** and **to the right**. **Release** the **mouse button**.

6. **Click** on the **first anchor** again (remember, a small circle appears on the pointer you reach the first anchor). Your completed object will be a heart shape with two curved anchors and two corner anchors.

7. **Command+click** on a **blank area** of the artboard. The object is deselected.

4

Selecting and Manipulating Objects

All right! You have an image on the paper. Now it needs some tweaking. Maybe the curves aren't exactly right or some of the line segments are too short or too long. Or it isn't in the right position. It needs help! The beauty of creating art on the computer is that nothing is permanent until you say so. The following pages show you how to use the selection tools to rearrange, delete, duplicate, push, pull, twist, twirl, wrangle, and otherwise harass your images into exactly what or where you want them to be. In this chapter you'll learn how to …

- Select, edit, move, and delete an object
- Duplicate or copy and paste an object
- Select and group multiple objects
- Select an anchor or a portion of an object
- Add, delete, join, or change anchor points
- Edit a path

Using the Selection Tools

Using a selection tool is like attaching a handle to an object or an anchor point so that you can drag it to its proper position. When selecting an anchor point, these selection handles actually sprout from the object so you can tweak the curve or angle. It takes a little practice, but soon you'll be selecting and manipulating objects in your sleep. If you still have the heart object from the last chapter on your screen, good. If you don't, go ahead and make another one—we'll use it for these demonstrations.

Selecting an Object

You always have to select an object before you can do anything to it. It seems simple now, but when you have a complex illustration with hundreds or thousands of objects of different sizes and on different layers, selecting one particular object might not be as easy as you think! Fortunately, Illustrator provides a variety of ways to select an object.

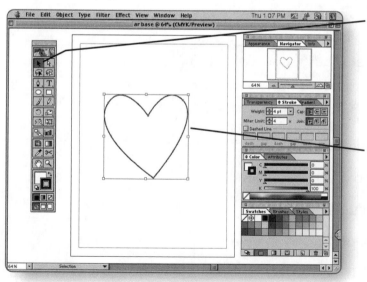

1. **Click** on the **Selection tool**. The tool will become active.

2. **Move** the **pointer** over the object until a small, black square appears below the pointer, and then **click**.

A wire-frame outline and a bounding box will appear around the object, indicating that the object is selected.

Deleting an Object

You can quickly delete an object you no longer need.

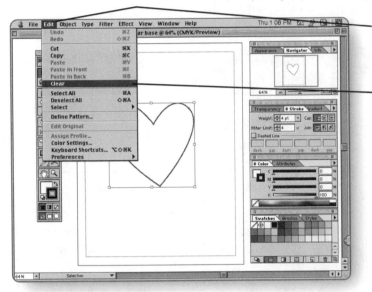

1. With the object selected, **click** on **Edit**. The Edit menu will open.

2. Click on **Clear**. The menu will close and the selected object will be deleted.

TIP

Pressing the Delete key on the keyboard will also delete the selected object.

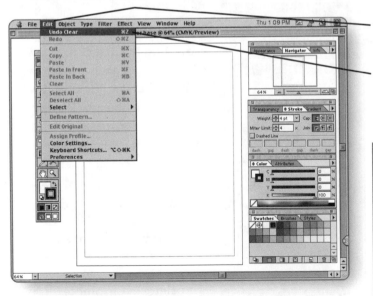

3. Click on **Edit**. The Edit menu will open.

4. Click on **Undo Clear**. The menu closes and the object returns to the screen.

TIP

If you make a mistake, just click on Edit, Undo. You can undo up to 200 times, depending on the memory available in your computer. The Edit menu always reflects what step is next to be undone.

To reverse an Undo command, select Edit, Redo.

Moving an Object

If an object is not where you want it, you can always move or reposition it elsewhere on the artboard.

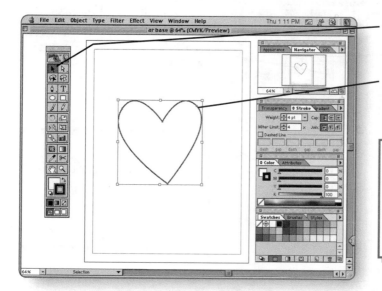

1. **Click** on the **Selection tool**. It will become active.

2. **Click** on the **object**. It will be selected.

TIP

Press an arrow key to nudge a selected object just a smidge up, down, left, or right.

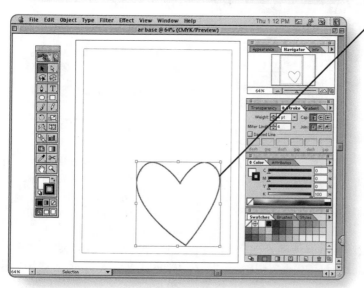

3. **Drag** the **object** to a new location, and then **release** the **mouse button**. The object will reappear in the new location.

NOTE

You can use the Transform palette to enter precise X (horizontal) and Y (vertical) points for an object. You'll learn more about the Transform palette in Chapter 5, "Transforming Objects."

Copying and Pasting an Object

At times, you will want an exact duplicate of your object. If so, just copy your object to the Clipboard and then paste it on the artboard.

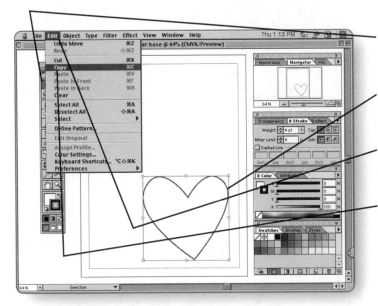

1. **Click** on the **Selection tool.** It will become active.

2. **Click** on the **object**. It will be selected.

3. **Click** on **Edit.** The Edit menu will open.

4. **Click** on **Copy.** A copy of the object will be temporarily stored in the Clipboard.

CAUTION

You won't actually see the Clipboard or its contents—it works in the background. You can reuse a Clipboard item as many times as you like, but remember that the Clipboard only provides temporary storage. The next time you choose Copy or Cut, you'll overwrite the existing Clipboard contents. The Clipboard will also be erased when you exit Illustrator.

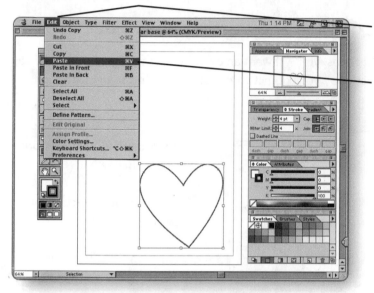

5. **Click** on **Edit** again. The Edit menu will open.

6. **Click** on **Paste**. A new wireframe will be placed on the artboard that is identical to and slightly offset from the original object.

NOTE

The Edit menu also has commands for pasting the duplicate directly in front of or in back of the original. As you experiment with the program, you'll find that this is a very nice option for creating multiple outline colors and other effects.

Copy by Dragging

Another way to duplicate an object is to hold down the Option key while you click and drag a copy off of the original.

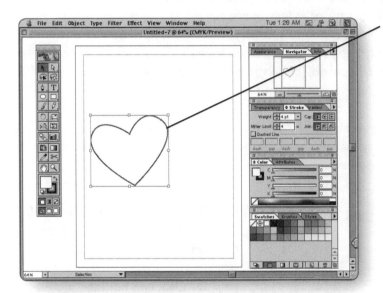

1. **Press and hold** the **Option key** as you **move** the **Selection tool** over the selected object. A small white arrowhead will appear next to the pointer.

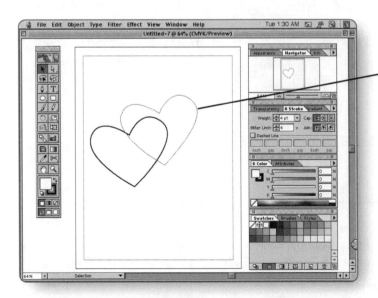

2. **Click** on the **object** and **drag** it in **any direction**.

The duplicate will be dragged off the top of the first object.

3. **Release** the **mouse button**, and then **release** the **Option key**. Repeat as often as needed.

Selecting and Grouping Multiple Objects

When your illustration gets more detailed, it's sometimes necessary, or at least more convenient, to group two or more objects together so that you can work with them as one unit. Any commands or settings applied to a group will affect all individual objects in the group even if they otherwise have different characteristics.

Duplicate an object using one of the earlier methods in this chapter, and then use the following steps to group them together.

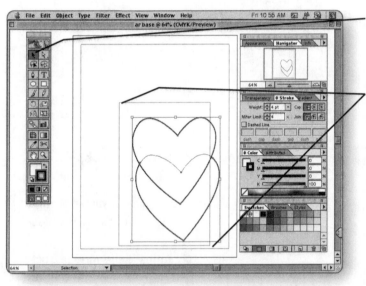

1. Click on the **Selection tool**. The Selection tool will become active.

2. **Click and hold** the **mouse button** while you drag the pointer across all of the objects you want to select. All the objects you touched will be selected in a single bounding box.

NOTE

Press Command+A to select all objects in the drawing, or press Command+Shift+A to deselect everything.

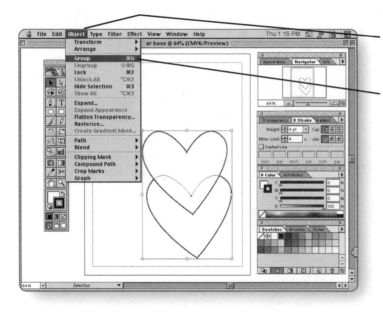

3. Click on **Object**. The Object menu will open.

4. Click on **Group**. The objects will be grouped so you can manipulate them as a single unit.

TIP

You can individually select multiple objects for grouping by holding down the Shift key and clicking on the objects one at a time. This method is particularly useful when you have smaller objects inside the grouping area that you want to exclude, or anytime you want to be picky with your selections.

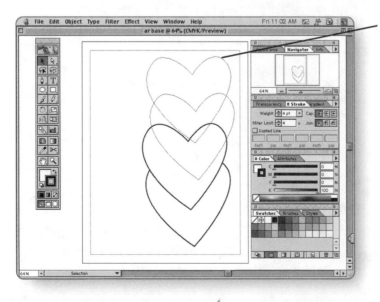

5. Drag the **group** to a **new location** on the artboard. Notice that all of the items in the group move without changing their location relative to each other.

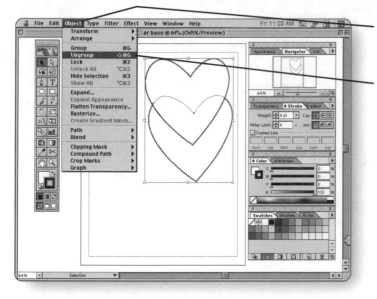

6. **Click** on **Object**. The Object menu will open.

7. **Click** on **Ungroup**. The selected grouped objects will ungroup, and the menu will close. You can now manipulate the objects independently.

Selecting an Anchor Point

No matter how good you get at drawing an object in Illustrator, you will need to know how to edit the individual anchor points. We'll use the heart shape again.

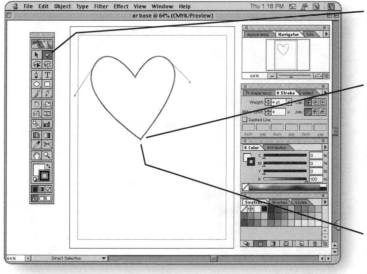

1. **Click** on the **Direct Selection tool**. The tool will become active.

2. **Move** the **pointer** to the **bottom point** of the heart. A black box will appear to the right of the pointer. When the pointer is exactly over a selectable anchor point, the little black box will turn white.

3. **Click** on the **anchor point**. The point will be selected.

Selecting Multiple Anchor Points

The following steps demonstrate how to select more than one anchor point at a time.

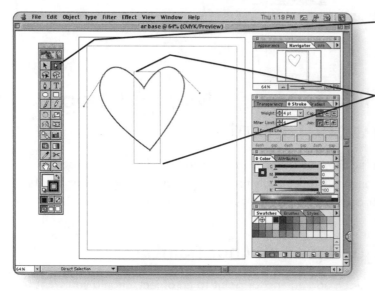

1. **Click** on the **Direct Selection tool**. The tool will become active.

2. **Click and drag** diagonally over the **upper and lower corner points** in the heart. A dotted-line *marquee* will appear, indicating the area you've included in the selection so far.

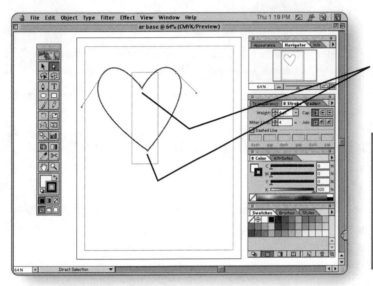

3. **Release** the **mouse button**. The marquee will disappear.

The two corner anchor points will be selected and the two curve points remain unselected.

TIP

You also can select multiple anchor points by holding down the Shift key while clicking on the individual points.

Selecting and Manipulating Anchor Points

In addition to the tools you've seen so far, the Pen tool palette includes tools for adding and deleting anchor points or converting a corner point to a curve (or vice versa).

Adding an Anchor Point

You can add an anchor point to an object, should you want to further manipulate it.

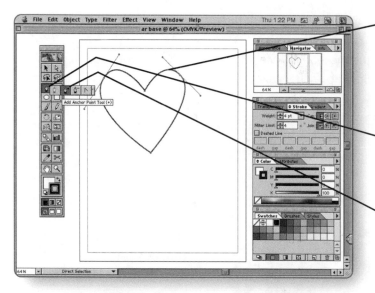

1. **Click** on the **heart-shaped object** from the preceding section (or create a new heart) if necessary. The object will appear as a selected wireframe.

2. **Click and hold** the **mouse button** over the Pen tool. A pop-up palette will appear.

3. **Point** to the **Add Anchor Point tool** and **release** the **mouse button**. The tool will become active and replace the Pen tool in the oolbox.

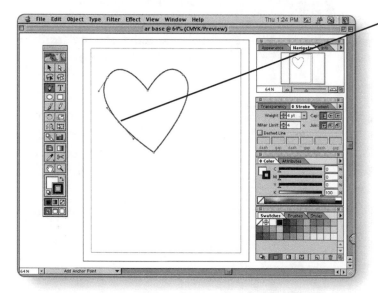

4. **Click** on **any segment** of a selected path. A new anchor point will appear on the path at the point where you clicked.

Deleting an Anchor Point

If the malleability of your object is vexing you, you can easily delete an anchor point or two.

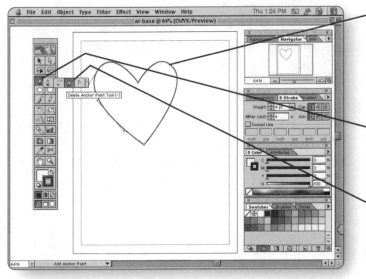

1. **Click** on the **heart-shaped object** from the preceding section (or create a new one) if necessary. The object will appear as a selected wireframe.

2. **Click and hold** the **mouse button** over the Pen tool. A pop-up palette will appear.

3. **Point** to the **Delete Anchor Point tool** and **release** the **mouse button**. The tool will become active and replace the Pen tool in the toolbox.

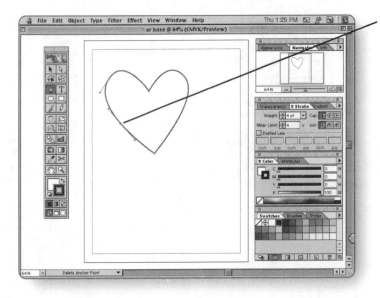

4. **Click** on **any anchor point**. The anchor will be removed from the path, and the object will be reshaped accordingly.

Converting an Anchor Point

The Convert anchor point tool on the Pen palette enables you to transform an anchor from a curve point to a corner point, or vice versa. This is a good method to use when you want to change the fundamental shape of an object in a hurry.

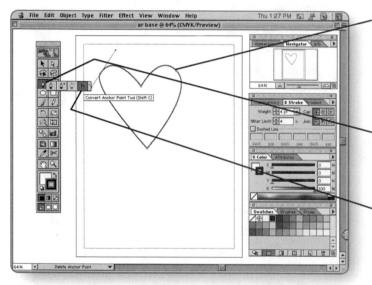

1. Click on the **heart-shaped object** from the preceding section (or create a new one) if necessary. The object will appear as a selected wireframe.

2. Click and hold the mouse button over the Pen tool. A pop-up palette will appear.

3. Point to the Convert Anchor Point tool and release the mouse button. The tool will become active and replace the Pen tool in the toolbox.

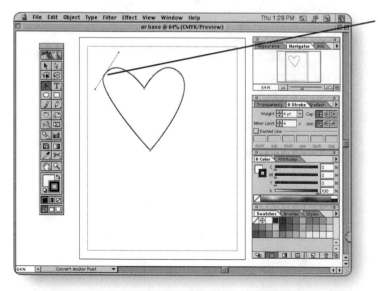

4. Click on a curved anchor point.

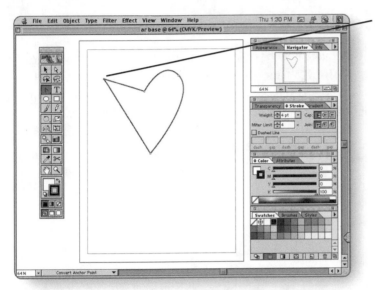

The curved anchor will convert to a corner anchor and the object will be reshaped.

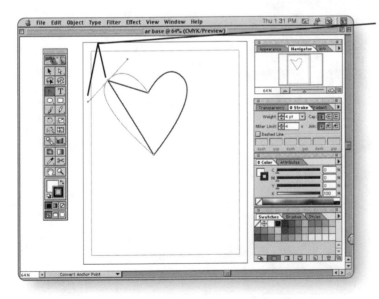

5. **Click and drag** on the **corner point** with the Convert anchor point tool. The corner point will be converted back to a curve point, and the object will be reshaped.

Editing a Path

After you've selected an anchor point, you can use the Direct selection tool to move anchor points or change the radius of the curve on a path.

NOTE

For more information on paths, see Chapter 8, "Using Color, Strokes, and Fills."

Moving an Anchor Point

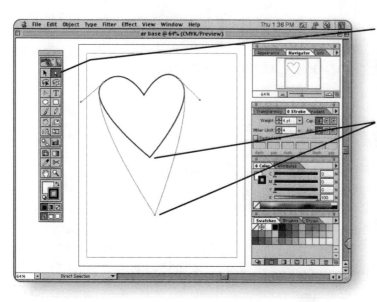

1. Click on the **Direct Selection tool**. The Direct Selection tool will become active.

2. Click and drag downward on the bottom corner anchor point on the heart.

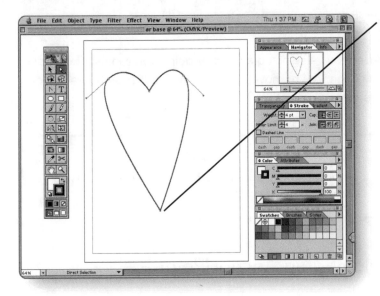

3. **Release** the **mouse button**. The anchor point will be moved to the new location, and the heart shape will be elongated.

Editing a Curved Anchor

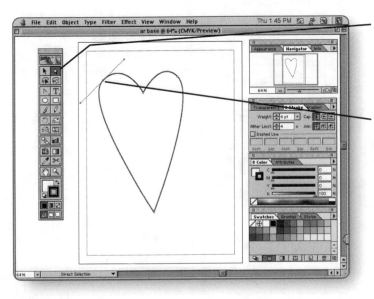

1. **Click** on the **Direct Selection tool**. The Direct-Selection tool will become active.

2. **Click** on a **curved anchor point**. The point will be selected and the direction lines with the direction points will become visible.

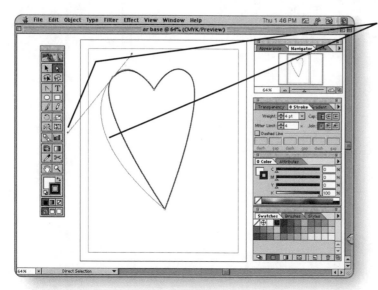

3. Click on the **lower direction point**, and then **drag downward and to the left**. The left side of the heart will bulge to the left.

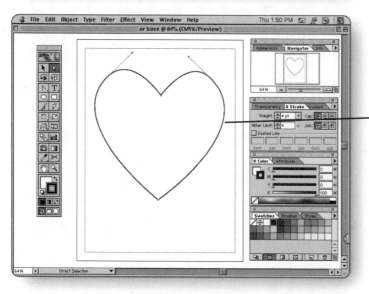

4. **Release** the **mouse button**. The object will be redrawn. Repeat steps 2-4 on the right side of the heart.

5. Keep moving and pulling the **anchor and direction points** until the heart looks the way you want it.

NOTE

Getting a feel for editing the paths just takes some practice. As you work with the anchor points and the Direct selection tool, it all becomes more intuitive, and at some point you'll find that it's no more complicated than using a pencil. And you won't need an eraser!

5

Transforming Objects

Illustrator's Transform tools enable you to change an object's size, shape, position, location, or perspective. You can even transform or "blend" one object into another. In this chapter, you'll learn how to …

- Rotate an object
- Resize an object
- Create a mirror image of an object
- Skew the angle of an object
- Use the Free Transform tool
- Blend two objects together

Using the Rotate Tools

With the Rotate tool, you can spin an object around on its center or select any other point on the artwork to be the center of the rotation. Like most other tasks in Illustrator, you can do the same thing with more than one tool or procedure, but the steps shown here are the easiest and most commonly used.

NOTE

If you're working with grouped objects, remember that all objects in the group will be transformed in the same way, even if they are differently shaped objects.

Rotating an Object

Before you can work with an object, you must have one on the artboard. Go ahead and draw a polygon (multisided object) of some kind now—the type is unimportant, because the tools treat all objects similarly. I'll use a star shape for the examples in this chapter.

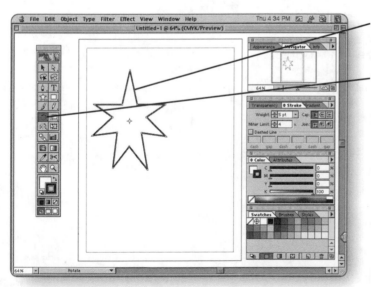

1. Select the object using any of the selection methods.

2. Click on the Rotate tool. The Rotate tool will become active, and a rotation center point will appear within the object.

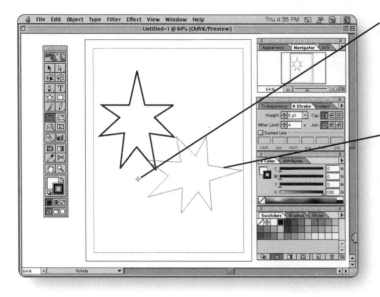

3. Click anywhere on the page to change the rotation center point. The center point will move to the location where you clicked.

4. Click and drag the object in any direction around the center point until it rotates to the desired position. As you drag, a wireframe of the object will show the results of your actions.

5. Release the mouse button and deselect the object. The object appears in its new position.

Rotating an Object Precisely

Most of the Transform tools also provide a way to perform a more specific transformation. The following steps explain how to rotate a selected object to a specific angle.

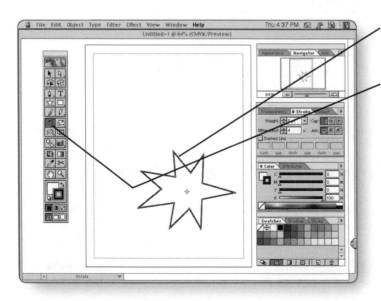

1. Select the object using any of the selection methods.

2. Double-click on the Rotate tool. The Rotate dialog box will appear, and the rotation center point will appear in the object.

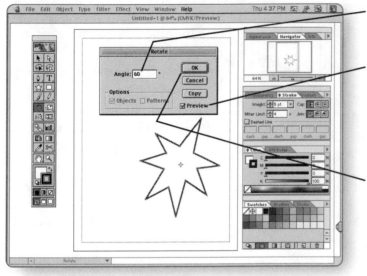

3. Enter the desired angle in the Angle text box.

4. Select the Preview check box. The object will rotate to the position entered. If it's not as desired, repeat steps 3 and 4 until the angle is just right.

5. Click on OK. The dialog box will close and the object will be rotated.

NOTE

You can enter any number between 0.00° and 360.00° into the Rotate dialog box. You can use a negative number to rotate the object counterclockwise, but it's no different than rotating it clockwise with the opposite measurement. (270° is the same thing as -90°).

TIP

Click on the Copy button in the Rotate dialog box to create a rotated copy of the object and leave the original object unchanged.

Using the Resizing Tools

Very rarely will you draw an object exactly the size and shape you want (unless you use a precision entry to create the object) right off the bat. You should know how to resize an object, because you will likely do it frequently. Fortunately, it's a very easy process.

Resizing an Object

To enlarge or reduce the size of an object, use the Scale tool. Select an object with the Selection or Lasso tool, and then do the following.

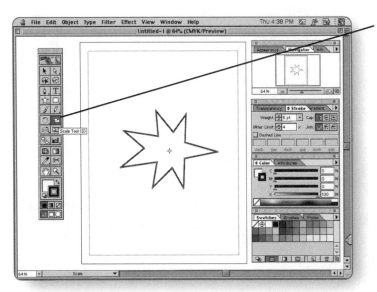

1. **Click** on the **Scale tool**. The Scale tool will become active, and a point of origin will appear in the object. The object will resize from this point.

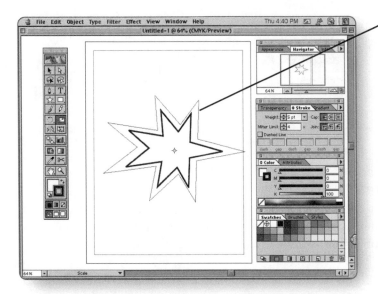

2. **Click anywhere** and **drag away** from the point of origin to grow the object. (Drag toward the point to shrink the object.)

TIP

Hold down the Shift key while dragging diagonally to maintain proportionate dimensions of the object while you scale it.

Resizing an Object Precisely

The Scale tool also has a dialog box for resizing an object to exact percentages. Select an object and perform the following steps to resize with the Scale dialog box.

1. **Double-click** on the **Scale tool**. The Scale dialog box will appear and a point of origin will appear in the center of the object.

2. **Click** on the **Uniform option button** to scale the object proportionally.

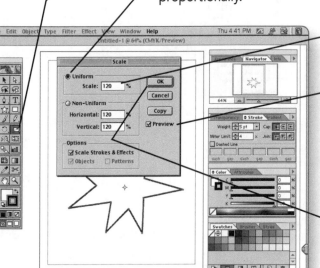

3. **Enter** a **percentage value** in the Scale text box.

4. **Click** in the **Preview check box**. Illustrator will show the proposed resized object. If the size change is the way you want it, uncheck the Preview check box.

5. **Click** on **OK**. The dialog box will close and the selected object will be resized proportionally.

TIP

Click on the Scale Strokes & Effects check box to maintain a proportional stroke thickness on the object.

If you click on the Non-Uniform radio button in the Scale dialog box and enter different numbers in the Horizontal and Vertical text boxes, you will distort the object in two directions. Enter negative numbers to flip the object.

Changing Orientation and Perspective

What if you have an object that's the right size and shape, but it's not facing the right way, or you'd like to give it a different perspective? As luck would have it, Illustrator thought of that, too, and made it just a few clicks' work.

Reflecting an Object

When you need to show a mirror image or create the opposite side of a complex object, you'll want to use the Reflect tool. Create an object you want to reflect, and select it with the Selection or Lasso tool before you begin these steps. For this example, I used a Christmas tree-like shape.

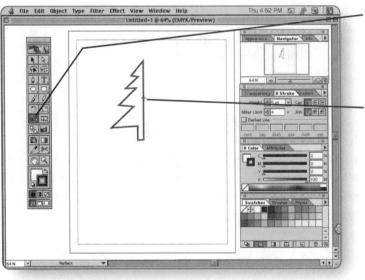

1. Click on the **Reflect tool**. The Reflect tool will become active, and a point of origin will appear on the object.

2. Click on the **right side** of the object to relocate the point of origin. This point will be the axis across which the reflection will flip.

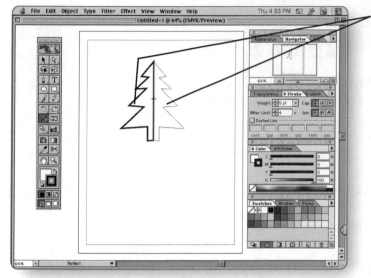

3. Move the **pointer** to the left side of the object, and then **click and drag horizontally** across the object. A wireframe of the object will flip across the point of origin.

4. Release the **mouse button**. The object will appear reversed from its original position.

5. Press **Command+z**. The object will return to its original position.

TIP

If you press the Option key *after* you start dragging, you will create a reflected copy of the object. The original will remain unchanged.

Reflecting an Object Precisely

At this point, you probably won't be surprised to find that the Reflect tool also offers a dialog box that you can use to reflect or flip an object to any specified angle. Before you begin the procedure, select the object to be reflected.

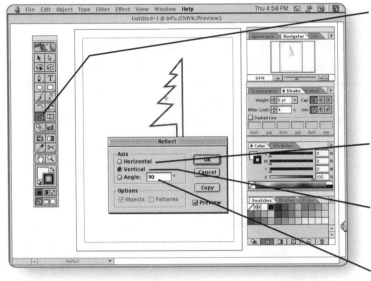

1. **Double-click** on the **Reflect tool**. The Reflect dialog box will appear.

2. **Click** on one of the following **Axis option buttons**:

• **Horizontal** will flip the object 90 degrees across the horizontal axis.

• **Vertical** will flip the object 90 degrees across the vertical axis.

• **Angle** will show the reflection at a specified angle; enter a number between 360 and –360 in the accompanying text box.

NOTE

Remember that because you're working with a reflection, negative numbers will flip the object clockwise, positive numbers counterclockwise. It's normally the other way around.

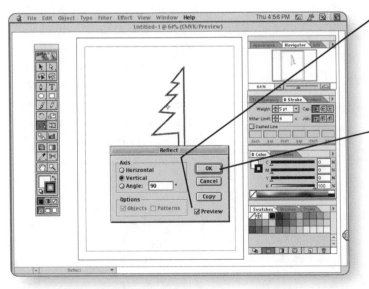

3. **Click** in the **Preview check box**. Illustrator will demonstrate the predicted results on the artboard. Repeat steps 2 and 3 as needed.

4. **Click** on **OK**. The dialog box will close and the selected object will be reflected.

Shearing an Object

The Shear tool is used to *skew* or slant an object across a point of origin. This tool can come in handy when you want to give an object some perspective. Begin by choosing an object and selecting it with the Selection or Lasso tool.

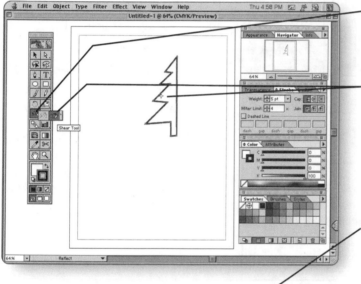

1. Click and hold the mouse button on the Reflect tool. The pop-up palette will appear.

2. Point to the Shear tool and release the mouse. The Shear tool will become active, and a point of origin will appear on the object.

3. Click anywhere on the artboard to move the point of origin to the desired location.

4. Click and drag from left to right to skew the object horizontally (or from top to bottom to skew vertically). Release the mouse button. The selected object will be skewed at an angle. Leave the object selected for the next exercise.

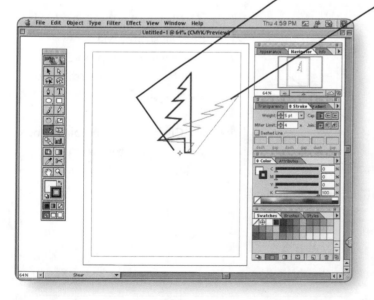

NOTE

Holding down the Option key before you start dragging will skew a copy of the object.

Skewing an Object

The Shear tool also offers a dialog box for preselecting the angle at which to skew the object. Make sure the object is selected with the Selection tool or the Lasso tool.

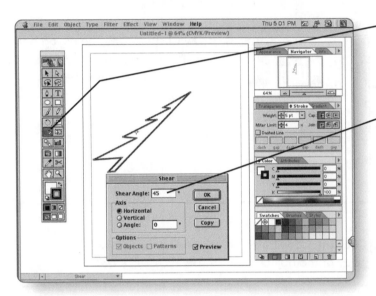

1. Double-click on the **Shear tool**. The Shear dialog box will appear and a point of origin will appear in the object.

2. Click in the **Shear Angle text box** and **enter** a **value** between 360 and –360 to specify the angle of the slant of the object.

3. Click on one of the **Axis option buttons** to skew the object along a horizontal or vertical plane:

- **Horizontal** will flip the object 90 degrees across the horizontal axis.

- **Vertical** will flip the object 90 degrees across the vertical axis.

- **Angle** will shows the skew at a specified angle; enter a number between 360 and –360 in the accompanying text box.

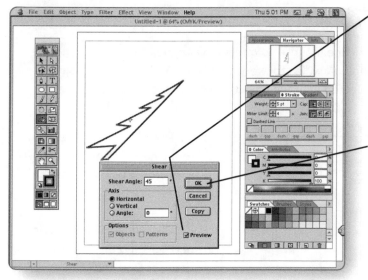

4. Click in the **Preview check box**. Illustrator will demonstrate the shear results on the artboard. Repeat steps 3 and 4 to tweak the shear to your liking.

5. Click on **OK**. The dialog box will close and the selected object will be skewed to the desired angle.

TIP

Click the Copy button in the Shear dialog box to skew a copy of the object.

Using the Free Transform Tool

With the Free Transform tool you can perform all of the transformations you just learned, but you also can distort an object or create perspective on only one side or corner of the object at a time. To explore this cool tool, create an object and select it with either the Selection tool or the Lasso tool. Then follow the steps in the following sections.

Free Transform Rotating

Use the Free Transform tool to rotate an object to literally any angle in one easy motion.

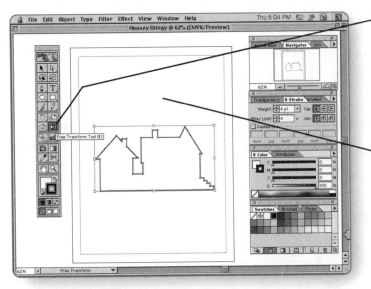

1. **Click** on the **Free Transform tool**. The tool will become active, and a bounding box with eight selection points, or handles, will surround the object.

2. **Point** just **outside** the object's wireframe. The pointer will change into a small, curved, double-headed arrow.

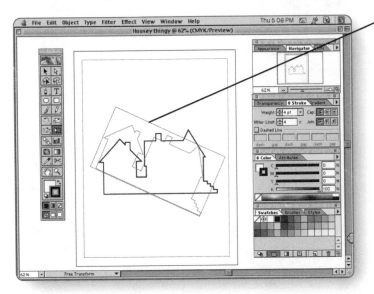

3. **Click and drag** around the **artboard** while holding down the mouse button. A wireframe of the object will rotate from its center point.

4. **Release** the **mouse button**. The object will appear in its new position.

NOTE

The Free Transform tool doesn't allow you to move the point of origin as the other Transform tools do. All of the operations with the Free Transform tool originate from the center of the object.

Free Transform Scaling

The Free Transform tool also comes in handy for quickly resizing or scaling an object.

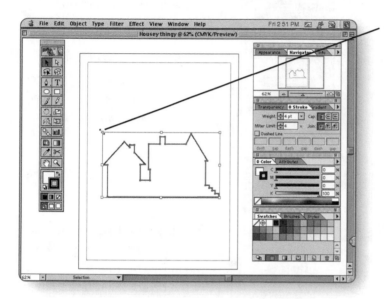

1. **Click and hold** on a **bounding box handle**. The pointer will change into a double-headed arrow.

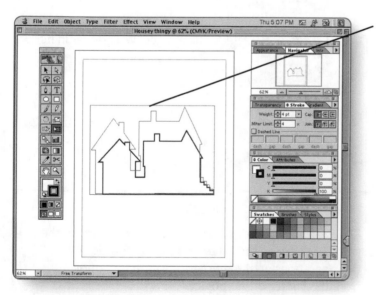

2. **Drag** the **mouse** in any direction. A wireframe will show the proposed new object dimensions.

3. **Release** the **mouse button**. The object will be resized both horizontally and vertically.

TIP

To constrain the object to its original proportions, hold down the Shift key before you start dragging the mouse. If you want to resize the object from its center, hold down the Option key while you drag the mouse.

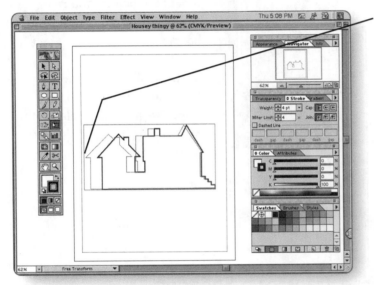

4. **Click and drag** on a **side handle** to resize the object horizontally.

5. **Release** the **mouse button**. The object will be rescaled in a single direction.

TIP

Click and drag on the top or bottom handle to resize the object vertically.

Free Transform Reflecting

Use Free Transform once again to flip an object and change its size at the same time.

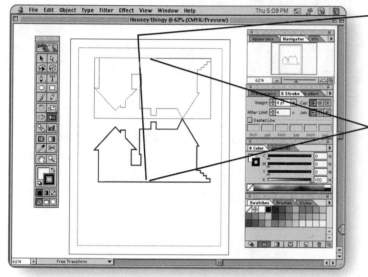

1. **Click** on the **handle** on the side to which you want to reflect the object. You can choose a side, top, or bottom handle.

2. **Drag** all the way **through the object** and **out the opposite side**; then **release** the **mouse button**. The object will be reversed.

Free Transform Shearing

Changing the object's skew on the fly is easy with the Free Transform tool, too. (Handy little tool, isn't it?)

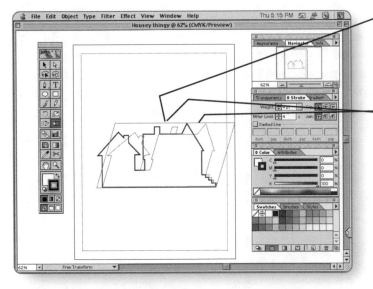

1. Click on the **bounding box handle** on the side you want to shear. You can choose a side, top, or bottom handle.

2. Press and hold the **Command key** and **drag** the **object** to the desired slant. A wireframe of the object will show the proposed changes.

3. Release the **mouse button** when the slant you want is achieved. The object will be skewed to the selected angle.

Distorting an Object

Here's where the Free Transform tool really shows its stuff. Select your object and make sure the tool is active before you begin.

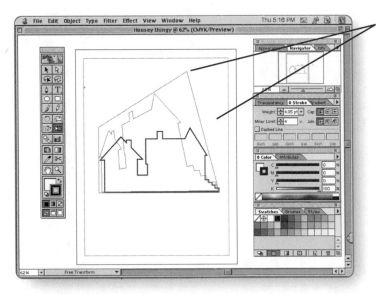

1. Click on a **corner handle** of the bounding box and **begin dragging**.

2. After you begin to drag, **press and hold** the **Command key**. You can drag the corner handle in any direction.

3. Release the **mouse button** at the desired position. The object will be distorted.

Applying Perspective

One red flag of a bad drawing is when it doesn't show the proper perspective. Fortunately, you've nothing to worry about. Illustrator makes it easy to create your object normally, and then apply the desired perspective so you don't end up with egg on your face.

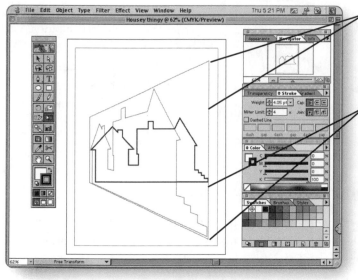

1. **Click** on a **corner handle** of the bounding box and begin dragging either horizontally or vertically.

2. After you begin to drag, **press and hold** the **Command, Option,** and/or **Shift keys.** The perspective will be maintained either vertically or horizontally along the line that you are dragging.

3. **Release** the **mouse button** at the desired position. The perspective will be applied along the horizontal or vertical line, depending on the direction in which you dragged in step 1.

Blending Two Objects

The Blend tool is a very powerful option in the toolbox, and it's also a lot of fun to experiment with. With the Blend tool, you can *blend* two or more objects together along a path: the object begins as one shape and gradually morphs into the other as the blend progresses. The shape and color of the objects change incrementally, as does the width of the stroke.

You can use blends to shade and highlight objects or to create the appearance of fades and shadows. In this exercise, we'll blend two geometric objects along a straight line. Before starting, create two objects of different color and shape.

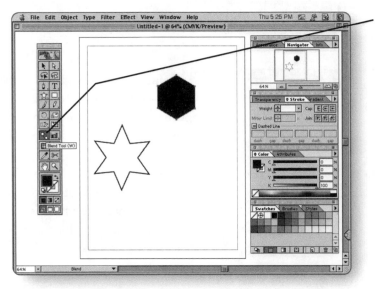

1. **Double-click** the **Blend tool**. The Blend Options dialog box will appear.

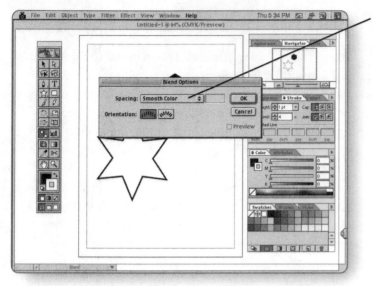

2. **Click and hold** on the **Spacing pop-up menu**. The menu will appear.

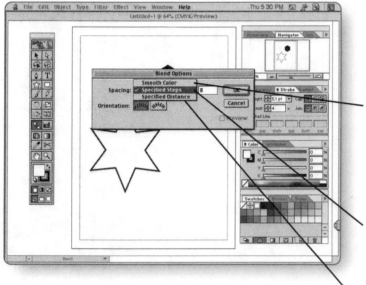

3. **Select** a **Spacing option** from the menu and enter an appropriate value in the text box:

- Click on **Smooth Color** to tell Illustrator to calculate and apply the number of steps between the two objects for a smooth, non-banded transition.

- Click on **Specified Steps** to choose the exact number of incremental steps for the blend.

- Click on **Specified Distance** to choose the incremental distance between steps.

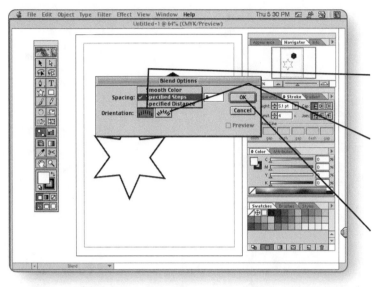

4. Click on an Orientation option:

- The left orientation box will align the blend objects perpendicular to the page.

- The right orientation box will align the blend objects perpendicular to the blend path.

5. Click on OK. The Blend Options dialog box will close.

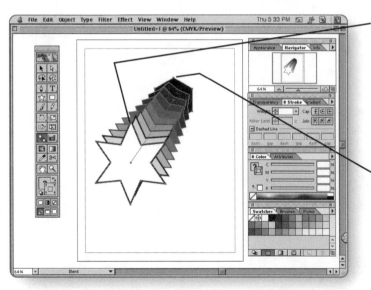

6. Locate a point on the first object. A small x will appear beside the tool when you are over an unselected point.

7. Click on the desired point. It will be selected.

8. Click on a point on the second object. Illustrator will calculate the blend and applies it along a blend path between the two objects.

NOTE

Blended objects need not be separated. You can place one object inside of another and blend for a great effect. You also can blend line widths and strokes from thick to thin or from one color to another.

6

Working with Precision

When you need to be exact, Illustrator gets down to the nitty-gritty with you. In Chapter 5, "Transforming Objects," you learned a few ways to control the placement and position of objects, but that was only the beginning! With rulers, guides, and grids at your disposal, you can measure the size of an object, set a specific distance between objects, and even place your objects precisely within the page—or in relation to each other. In this chapter, you will learn how to …

- Open and use the page rulers
- Create and move guides
- Open a grid
- Measure an object
- Move objects with the Transform palette
- Align and distribute objects on the page
- Move objects from front to back

Illustrator Rules!

To help you keep track of where you are on the page, Illustrator provides a pair of rulers you can display along the top and left side of the Illustrator window. Each ruler's zero point can be moved to coincide with any point on the artboard, so that you can use that spot as a beginning reference to measure any object or distance.

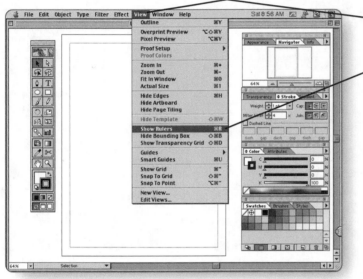

1. Click on **View**. The View menu will open.

2. Click on **Show Rulers**. The View menu will close, and two rulers will appear horizontally and vertically at the top and left of the art space.

NOTE

By default, the zeros on the rulers align with the lower left corner of the page. Also notice the dotted lines inside of the rulers that track the cursor as you move it around the page.

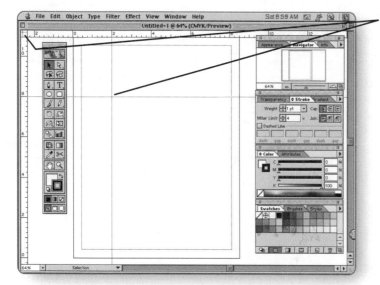

3. **Click** on the **corner box** where the two rulers intersect, and **drag** the **pointer** across the page. Intersecting dotted lines show you where on the current rulers the new zero point will be located.

4. **Release** the **mouse button.** The dotted lines disappear, and the zero points on the rulers align with the newly selected point on the page.

NOTE

All the measurements in this book are in inches. You can change the units of measure to points, picas, millimeters, centimeters, or pixels by using the Preferences dialog box. You'll learn more about setting Preferences in Appendix D, "Setting Preferences."

Using Guides

In addition to rulers along the edges of the window, you can place guides directly on your workspace. *Guides* are visible but nonprinting lines that you can use to precisely position or align objects on the page.

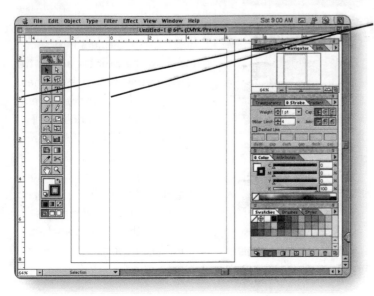

1. Click **anywhere** on the vertical ruler, **drag** to the **right**, into the page, and **release** the **mouse button**. A vertical guide will appear on the artboard.

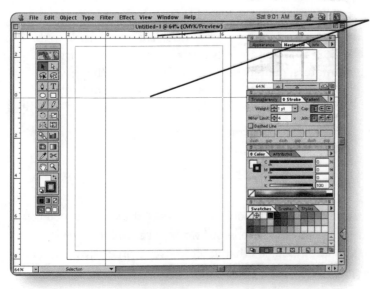

2. Click **anywhere** on the horizontal ruler, **drag down**, into the **page**, and **release** the **mouse button**. A horizontal guide will appear on the artboard.

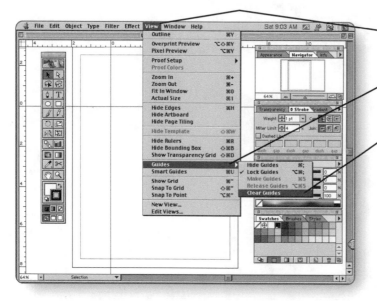

3. **Click** on **View**. The View menu will open.

4. **Point** to **Guides**. The Guides submenu will open.

5. **Click** on **Clear Guides**. The guides will be removed from the page.

Displaying the Grid

The *grid* is a framework of nonprinting lines that helps you place and arrange objects and lines in correct positions on the page. It's like graph paper for the screen.

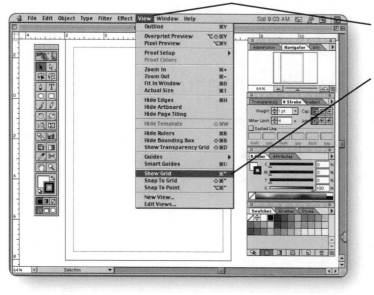

1. **Click** on **View**. The View menu will open.

2. **Click** on **Show Grid**. The menu closes, and the grid will appear onscreen.

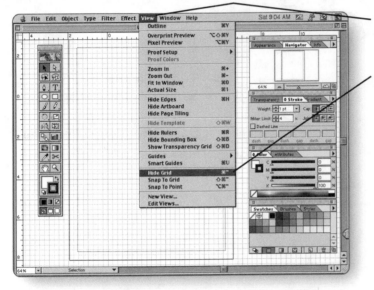

3. **Click** on **View**. The View menu will open.

4. **Click** on **Hide Grid**. The menu will close and the grid will disappear from view.

TIP

Enable the Snap To option on the View menu to "magnetize" the grid. The object will "snap" incrementally along the gridlines until it is in the precise position. This feature is handy when aligning objects. Snap to Grid works whether or not the grid is visible onscreen, and the grid can be visible without being magnetized.

Using the Measure Tool

For those times when you need to know the dimensions of an existing space or object, you can employ the Measure tool to accurately find any measurement on the artboard. But first you must create an object to measure.

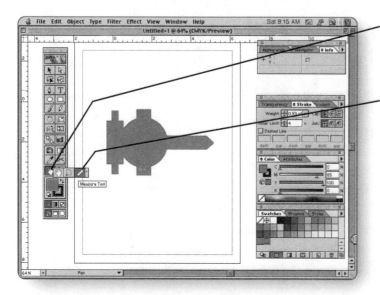

1. Click and hold on the Hand tool. A pop-up palette will appear.

2. Point to the Measure tool and release the mouse button. The Measure tool will become active.

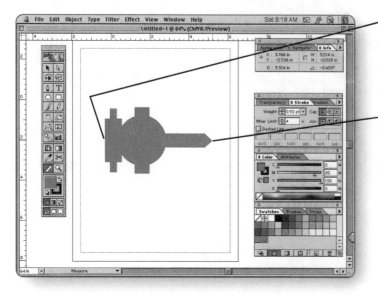

3. Click on the point at which you want to start the measurement. The Info palette will open.

4. Click on the point for the end measurement. The distance measurement will appear in the lower left corner of the Info palette (next to the D:).

TIP

After step 2, you also can click and drag between the two measuring points.

Moving and Sizing Objects Using the Transform Palette

The Transform palette can really come in handy if you need to move something a very short distance or to an exact location on the artboard. Create an object and select it before you try these steps.

NOTE

The first two steps aren't necessary if the palette is already open.

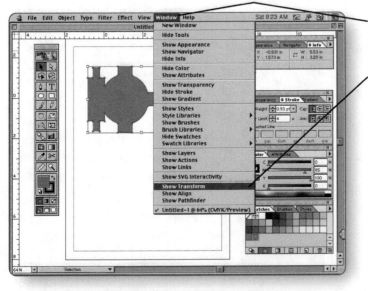

1. Click on **Window**. The Window menu will open.

2. Click on **Show Transform**. The Transform palette will appear.

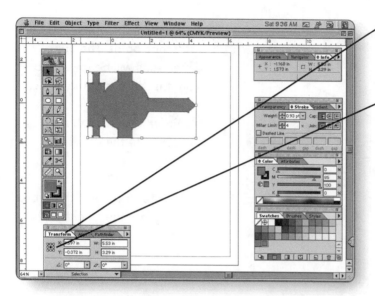

3. **Click** on the **Transform tab**. The Transform palette will come to the front.

4. **Click** on one of the nine **selection points** ("handles") to select it. These nine points represent the nine points of the bounding box that surrounds the object. The movement will be measured from that point and the intersecting point of origin made by the zeros on the rulers.

NOTE

Dragging by different handles (corner, side, top/bottom) produces somewhat different behaviors. You may want to experiment with each for a moment so you don't get unexpected results later.

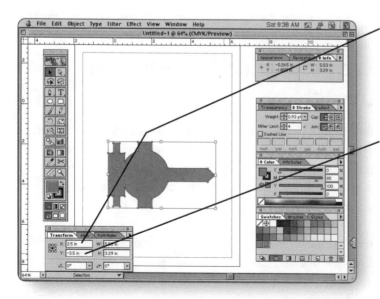

5. **Enter** a **value** in the X box to designate the distance to move horizontally. Higher numbers move the object to the right.

6. **Enter** a **value** in the Y box to designate the distance to move vertically. Higher numbers move the object up.

7. **Press Enter**. The object will move to the designated position.

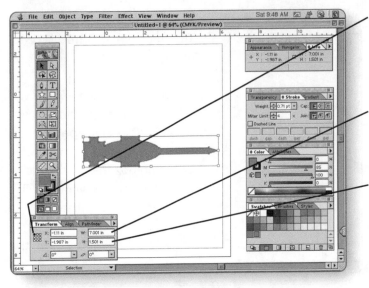

8. Click on the **upper left reference point**. The object's dimensions will be measured from that corner of the object.

9. Enter a **value** in the W box to designate the width of the object.

10. Enter a **value** in the H box to designate the height of the object.

NOTE

You can use the Transform palette to perform some of the same actions you learned about in Chapter 5—including rotations, skews, and scaling. I won't cover that here, because the palette tools work identically as those in the main toolbox.

Aligning and Distributing Objects

When you're working with several objects or lines and need to get them lined up or stacked along their common side or center, or if you need to distribute them along the page with some kind of regularity, the Align palette tools are great. This palette is one that I use constantly.

Create at least three different objects, and select them before you begin this section.

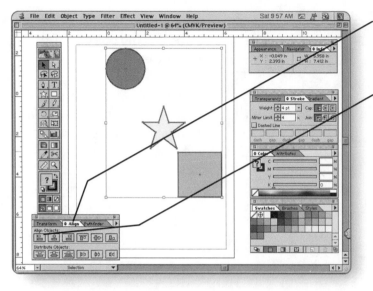

1. Click on the **Align tab**. The Align palette will move to the front.

2. Click on the **Horizontal Align Left** box. All the objects line up along their leftmost point.

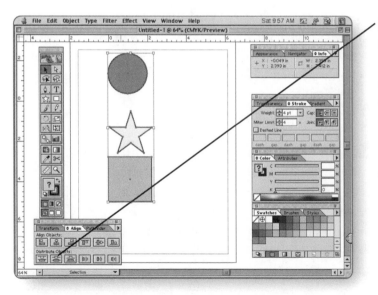

3. Click on the **Vertical Distribute Center** box. Illustrator calculates the average distance between the centers of the top and bottom objects and then moves the middle object so that its center is the equal distance between the centers of the other two.

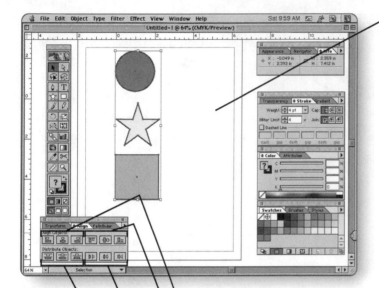

4. Click on a **blank area** on the artboard. The objects will be deselected.

Experiment with combining alignments to stack objects in front of each other. For example, clicking on Align Center Vertically and then Align Center Horizontally creates some interesting designs, depending on the shape and size of the objects and their order from front to back.

NOTE

In order from left to right across the top of the palette, the Align buttons will align objects:

- Vertically on the left side, through the center, or on the right side.
- Horizontally on the top, through the center, or on the bottom.

In order from left to right across the bottom of the palette, the Distribute buttons will distribute:

- Horizontally from the left, center, or right sides of the objects.
- Vertically from the tops, center, or bottoms of the objects, centers vertically, or the bottoms vertically.

Moving Objects from Front to Back

As you create objects on the page, you will notice that they sometimes overlap. All of the objects in a vector program are like cutout paper shapes stacked on top of each other. Every time you create a new object or line in Illustrator, that item is placed in front of, or on top of, all the others that were drawn before it. Sometimes you will need to rearrange or restack those items.

Before you try these steps, create three or more objects and overlap them on the page. Select the object in front—the object you drew last.

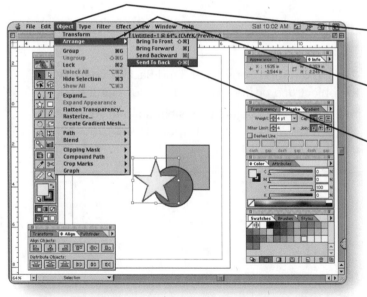

1. **Click** on **Object**. The Object menu will open.

2. **Point** to **Arrange**. The Arrange submenu will open.

3. **Click** on **Send To Back**. The menu will close, and the selected object will move to the back of the stack.

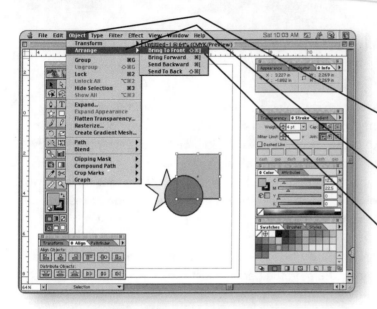

4. Click on one of the **rearward objects** with the **Selection** tool.

5. Click on **Object**. The Object menu will open.

6. Point to **Arrange**. The Arrange submenu will open.

7. Click on **Bring To Front**. The menu will close and the object will move to the front of the stack.

TIP

Clicking on Bring Forward or Send Backward will move the object one position forward or back in the stack.

You can select an object that is hidden behind another one by pressing Command+Option+[and clicking on the object.

7

Working with Paths and Pathfinders

In Chapter 4, "Selecting and Manipulating Objects," you learned how anchor points can help you manipulate and transform an object. Later you used the Selection tools to grab and move the objects around; then you distorted, stretched, and bent them with the Transform tools. Next, you will discover even more tricks for object morphing—welding objects together, cutting them up, bending and twisting them in amazing ways, and erasing them when you're done. Feel the power! In this chapter, you'll learn how to …

- Smooth, reshape, and erase objects
- Slice and dice objects using the Scissors and Knife tools
- Manipulate objects using the Join and Average commands
- Use the Pathfinder palette to create cool drawing effects

Using the Smooth Tool

The Smooth tool rounds and simplifies the shape of a curved path by deleting unnecessary points along the path. Before you start these steps, draw a rough curved path with the Pencil tool (something similar to the example will be fine). Be sure to leave the object selected.

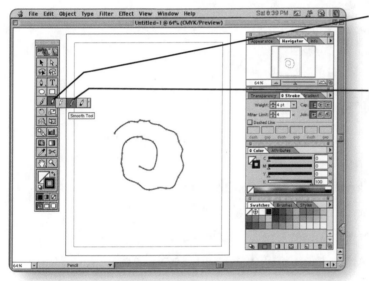

1. Click and hold on the Pencil tool. A pop-up palette will appear.

2. Move the pointer to the Smooth tool and release the mouse button. The Smooth tool will be activated.

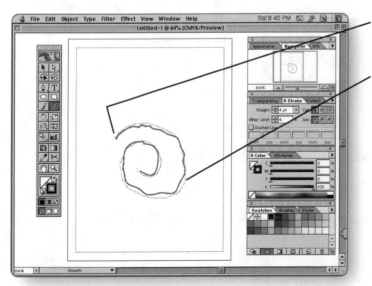

3. Move the Smooth tool pointer near the selected path.

4. Click and drag along the section you want to smooth. A dotted line will appear along the path you follow.

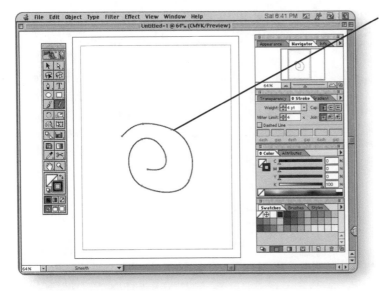

5. **Release** the **mouse button**. The dotted line will disappear along with all the unnecessary anchor points, creating a smooth, continuous curve.

Using the Eraser Tool

Hey, everybody makes mistakes. Here's the way you erase an unwanted section from a path without having to scrap the whole thing. For this example, use the curved line you just smoothed out, and select it with the Selection or Lasso tool.

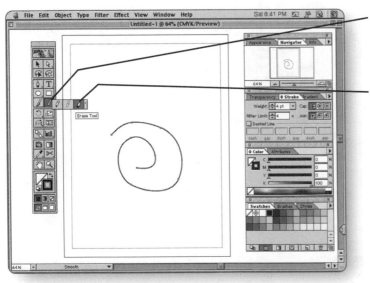

1. **Click and hold** the **mouse button** on whatever tool is in the Pencil tool area.

2. **Move** the **pointer** to the Erase tool and **release** the **mouse button**. The Erase tool will be activated, and the pointer will change to resemble a small eraser.

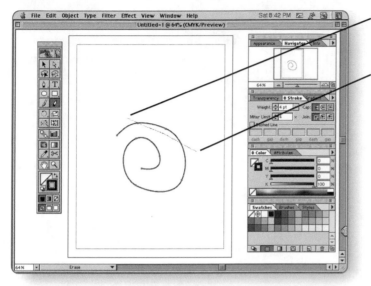

3. **Place** the **Erase tool pointer** on the path.

4. **Click and drag** the **pointer** along the section of the path that you want to erase. A dotted line will appear behind the eraser.

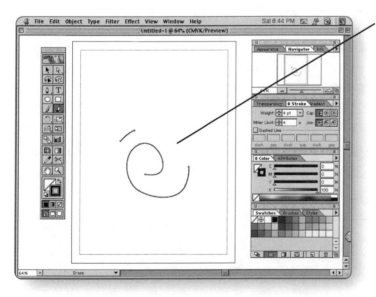

5. **Release** the **mouse button** at the ending point. The dotted line will vanish, along with the path section that you wanted to erase.

Using the Reshape Tool

The Reshape tool is used in places where you might want to stretch a segment of an object without distorting the whole thing. Draw an object that is not symmetrical and has a few complex angles and curves along the path. I'm using this fish cartoon, but any object will do.

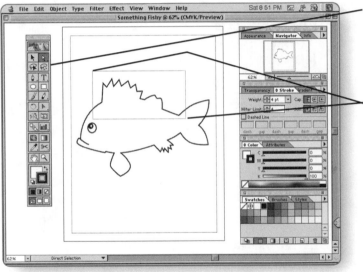

1. Click on the **Direct Selection tool**. (Alternatively, you could use the Direct Lasso tool.)

2. **Click and drag** a **marquee** to select some anchor points on one side of the object.

TIP

Use the Direct Selection tool and Shift+Click to select individual points.

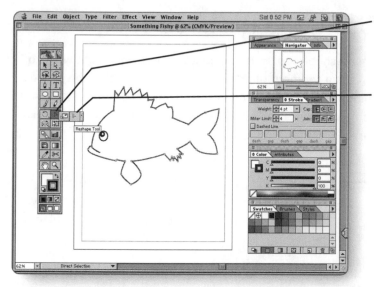

3. **Click and hold** on the **Scale tool**. A pop-up palette will appear.

4. **Drag** the **pointer** to the Reshape tool and release the mouse button. The Reshape tool will become active.

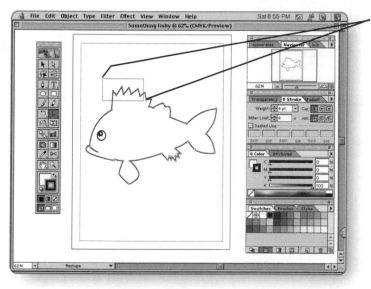

5. **Click and drag** around **some portion of the object.** A marquee will appear around the area.

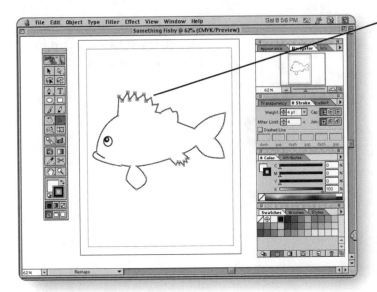

6. **Release** the **mouse button**. The marquee will disappear and small squares will appear around the selection points.

NOTE

You can click anywhere along the path with the Reshape tool, and a new anchor point will be placed there with the square around it.

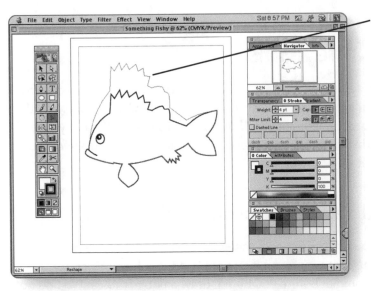

7. **Click** on **one of the squares** and **drag** in **any direction**. The object will stretch out using the first two nonselected points as anchors. The selected points will remain as they were in relation to each other.

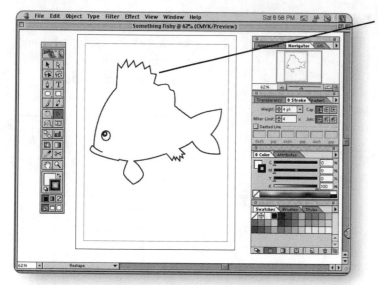

8. **Command+click** on **the object.** It will be reshaped to the new dimensions.

Using the Scissors and Knife Tools

One of the analogies people use when talking about a vector program such as Illustrator is that it's similar to working with cutout paper shapes. If that's the case, then it's no mystery why Illustrator calls these next tools Scissors and Knife: you cut objects with them.

Using the Scissors Tool

You use the Scissors tool when you want to split a path. It's the best way to cut a straight line though an object, for example. Before you begin, draw an object to cut. You do not need to select the object.

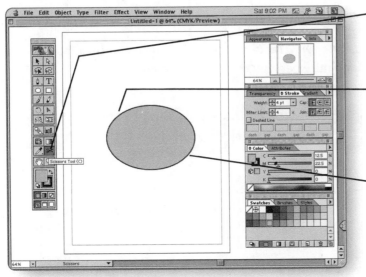

1. Click on the **Scissors tool**. The Scissors tool will be activated.

2. Click anywhere on the path to establish the first cut. A point will appear where you clicked.

3. Click elsewhere on the path to make the second cut. The object will split between the two cuts.

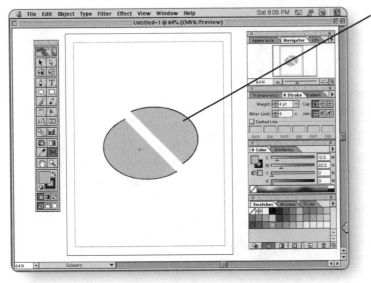

4. Command+click on **one segment**, and **drag** the **segments** apart. Notice that there is no path where the cut was made.

Using the Join Command

Illustrator will create a new line between two selected endpoints when you use the Join command.

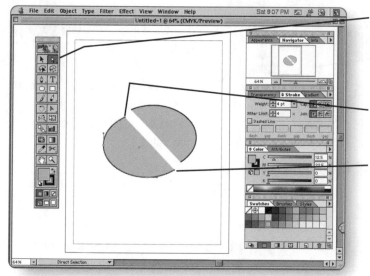

1. Click on the **Direct Selection tool**. The Direct-Selection tool will become active.

2. Click on one of the **endpoints**. It will be selected.

3. Shift+click on the **other endpoint**. It will be selected.

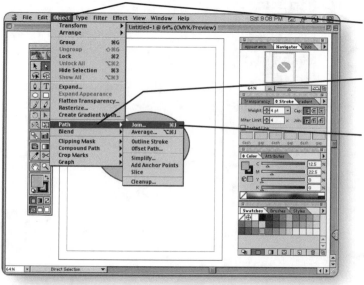

4. Click on **Object**. The Object menu will open.

5. Point to **Path**. The Path submenu will open.

6. Click on **Join**. The menus will close and a line will appear between the two selected paths.

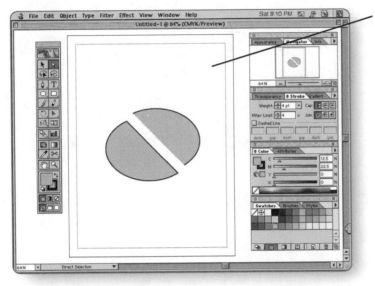

7. Command+click on an **empty place** on the artboard. The object will be deselected.

Using the Knife Tool

Use the Knife tool to slice chunks out of an object. Create an object to slice up.

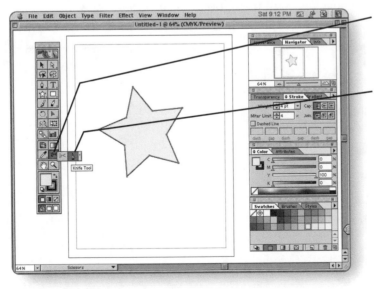

1. Click and hold on the **Scissors tool**. A pop-up palette will appear.

2. Move the **pointer** to the Knife tool and **release** the **mouse button**. The Knife tool will become active.

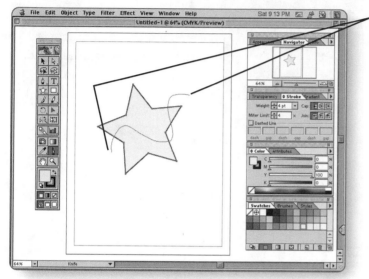

3. Click **anywhere outside** of the object and **drag** a **cut** through the object while holding the mouse button. As you drag, a line will appear indicating the cut.

CAUTION

The Knife tool will cut any object that happens to be in its way. If you are cutting an object that is on top of or overlapping another object, the knife will slice that other object as well. Use the Selection tool to select the object you want to cut before you begin. This will prevent you from cutting into other objects.

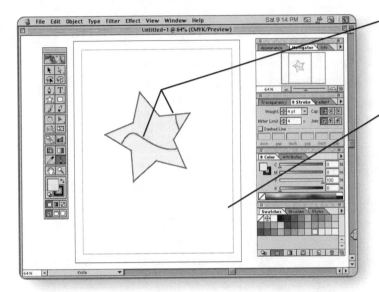

4. **Release** the **mouse button**. The line will disappear and the object will be cut along the desired path.

5. **Command+click** on an **empty place** on the artboard. The object will be deselected.

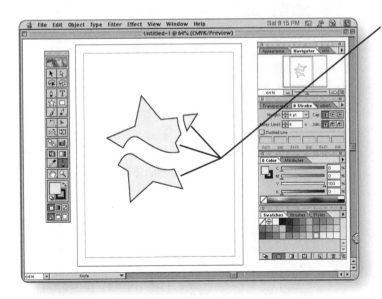

6. **Command+click** on the **severed pieces** one at a time, and **drag them** away from each other. Notice that there are three complete objects, each surrounded by a closed path.

Using the Average Command

The Average command works kind of like the Align tool, except that it aligns anchor points instead of whole objects. Use the Pen tool to draw a zigzag line on the artboard to get started.

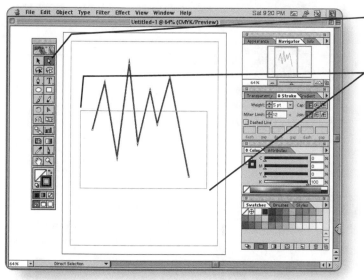

1. Click on the **Direct Selection tool** to make it active.

2. Click and drag a **marquee** around the lower anchor points to select them. (Or Shift+click to select individual points.) The marquee will appear in the area you indicated.

3. Release the **mouse button**. The points will be selected.

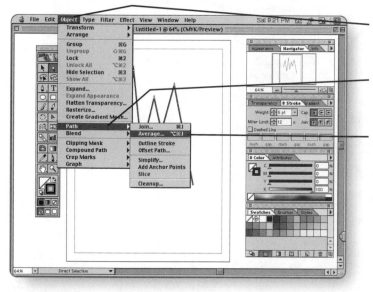

4. Click on **Object**. The Object menu will open.

5. Point to **Path**. The Path submenu will open.

6. Point to **Average** and release the **mouse button**. The menus will close and the Average dialog box will appear.

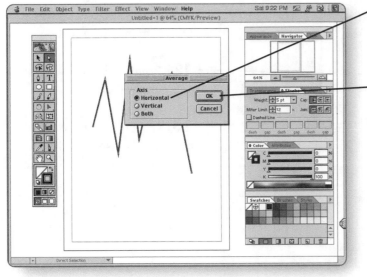

7. Click on **Horizontal** in the Axis area. The option will be selected.

8. Click on **OK**. The dialog box will close and the selected anchor points will be averaged along a horizontal plane.

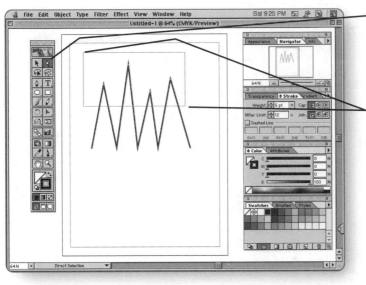

9. Click on the **Direct Selection tool** (if it's not already active). The Direct Selection tool will be activated.

10. Click and drag a marquee to select the upper anchor points. Release the mouse button. The points will be selected.

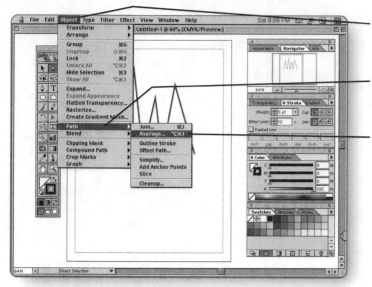

11. Click on **Object**. The Object menu will open.

12. Point to **Path**. The Path submenu will open.

13. Click on **Average**. The menus will close, and the Average dialog box will appear.

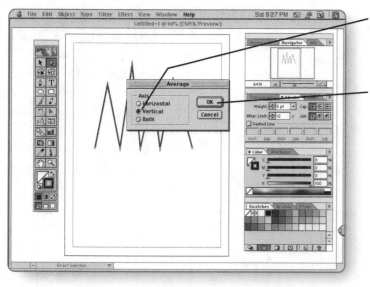

14. Click on **Vertical** in the Axis area. The option will be selected.

15. Click on **OK**. The dialog box will close and the upper anchor points will be averaged along a vertical plane.

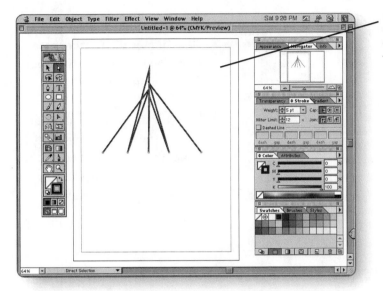

16. Command+click on an empty place on the artboard. The object will be deselected.

Closing a Path Using Average and Join

Often when you are working with very complex objects, it's hard to tell whether the object's path is open or closed. Often you'll find that the endpoints are overlapping but not joined. The best way to make sure that you have two endpoints in the correct position is to turn them into a single anchor point after you average them together. For the sake of illustration, we'll draw an open-ended path with endpoints that are obviously separated, average them, and then use the Join command to combine them into one anchor point.

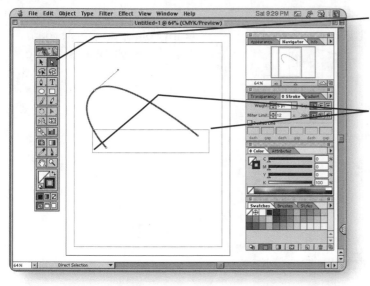

1. Click on the **Direct Selection** or the **Direct Lasso tool**. The Direct Selection tool will become active.

2. Click and drag a **marquee** around the two endpoints to select them. (Or Shift+click the endpoints.) Release the mouse button. The endpoints will be selected.

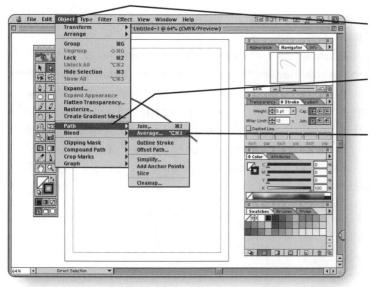

3. Click on **Object**. The Object menu will open.

4. Point to **Path**. The Path submenu will open.

5. Click on **Average**. The menus will disappear, and the Average dialog box will appear.

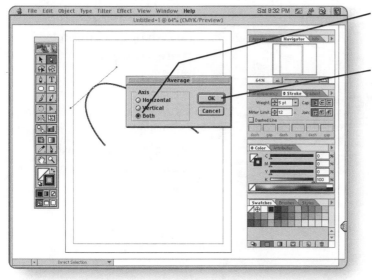

6. Click on **Both**. The option will be selected.

7. Click on **OK**. The dialog box will close and the two selected points will be averaged into the same position.

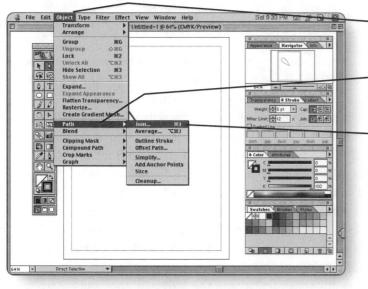

8. Click on **Object** again. The Object menu will open.

9. Point to **Path**. The Path submenu will open.

10. Click on **Join**. The menus will close, and a Join dialog box will appear.

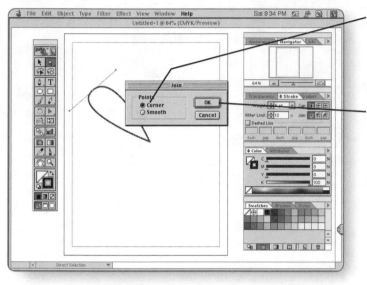

11. Select the Corner or Smooth option button to create a smooth or a corner point.

12. Click on OK. The dialog box will close and the two averaged end points will become one anchor point and close the path.

Using the Pathfinder Tools

The Pathfinder palette includes some of the most useful tools in Illustrator. These tools allow you to overlap objects and use them in conjunction with each other, so you can unite two or more simple objects and make something that's more complex. Or you can use one object as a cookie cutter to make it appear as though that object is in front of or behind the other object. Because the Pathfinder palette is a more advanced toolset, you're not likely to use it with very simple drawings. Before you begin these exercises, you'll need a minute to set up the scene: create two simple objects; give them different fill colors and no stroke. Arrange them so that they overlap each other. Select both objects, and copy and paste them five times onto the artboard. Distribute them so that you can work with one pair of objects at a time.

The Pathfinder palette contains 10 different tools divided into two rows of five. The upper row consists of the Combine tools. We'll start with those.

Using the Pathfinder Combine Tools

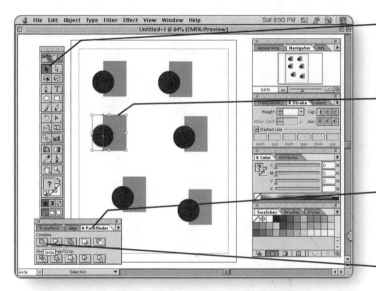

1. **Click** on the **Selection tool.** The Selection tool will become active.

2. **Click and drag** over one **pair of objects** to select them. (Or Shift+click on the individual objects.)

3. **Click** on the **Pathfinder tab.** The palette will come to the front.

4. **Click** on **Unite.** The two objects will become a single object, taking on the color attributes of the front object.

TIP

Click on Windows, Show Pathfinder if you need to open the Pathfinder palette before selecting the tab in step 3.

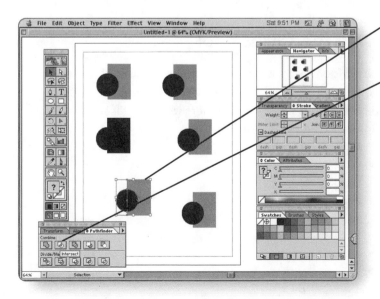

5. **Select** another **pair of objects** with the Selection tool.

6. **Click** on **Intersect.** The objects will disappear, leaving an object defining only the space where the two original objects intersected.

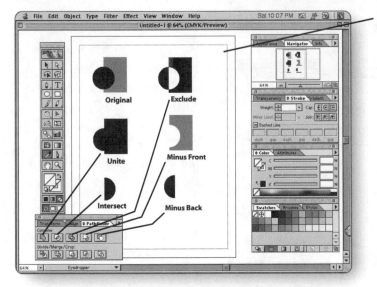

7. **Repeat** the **process** on the remaining pairs of objects until you understand all the buttons in the top row of the Pathfinder palette.

Using the Pathfinder Divide Tools

The Divide tools (Divide, Trim, Merge, Crop, and Outline) differ from the Combine tools in that they split the objects into grouped segments or trim and delete unnecessary segments of the objects.

Using the Divide Tool

The Divide tool makes individual shapes out of the overlapping areas of the objects. Create two overlapping objects for this exercise give them different fill colors and no stroke.

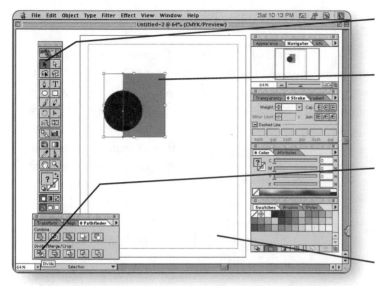

1. Click on the **Selection tool**. It will become active.

2. Click and drag over the **objects** to select them. (Or Shift+click on the individual objects.)

3. Click on **Divide** in the Pathfinder palette. The objects will be divided along their paths and grouped.

4. Click on an **empty place** on the artboard. The objects will be deselected.

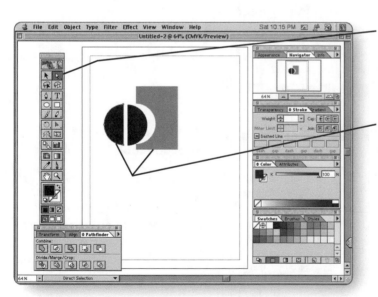

5. Click on the **Direct Selection tool**. The Direct Selection tool will become active.

6. Click inside **any of the sections** and **drag them** apart to see the results of the command.

Using the Trim Tool

The Trim tool works kind of like the Combine palette's Minus Front command—all the overlapping areas behind the front object will be eliminated. The difference is that the front object remains on the artboard. Re-create the objects, or use Undo (Command+Z) to restore the objects from the preceding exercise back to their original form. Then select both with the Selection or Lasso tool.

1. **Click** on **Trim** in the Pathfinder palette. The object in front will trim the rear object or objects, and the overlapping areas will be discarded.

2. **Click** on the **Direct Selection tool**. The tool will become active.

3. **Click and drag** on any of the **sections** to pull them apart.

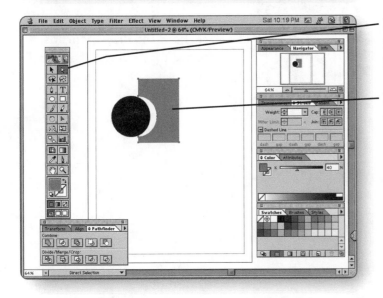

Using the Merge Tool

The Merge command will maintain the front object and unite it with any other overlapping object with the same fill. Other objects will be trimmed by the object in front of it. Whew! Got all that?

To set up this demonstration, re-create or revert the objects to their original forms; then add another object with a different shape and the same fill color as the front object. Overlap the objects and send the new object to the back.

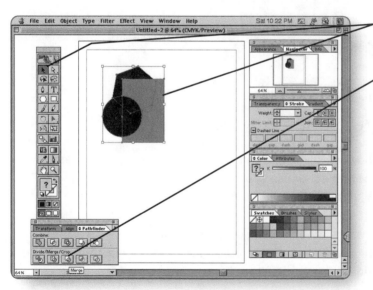

1. **Select** all of the **objects** with the Selection or Lasso tool.

2. **Click** on **Merge** in the Pathfinder palette. The front and rear objects will unite. The front object will trim the middle object, and the middle object will trim the rear object.

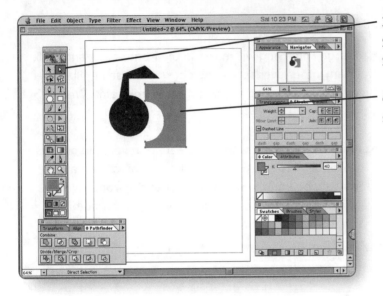

3. **Click** on the **Direct Selection tool**. The Direct-Selection tool will be active.

4. **Click and drag** on any **section** to move it.

Using the Crop Tool

The Crop command trims and discards everything that the front object doesn't cover. The fills from the underlying objects remain to replace the fill of the front object.

Use the same three objects we used in the Merge exercise. Re-create or revert the objects to their original form, but bring the new object to the front.

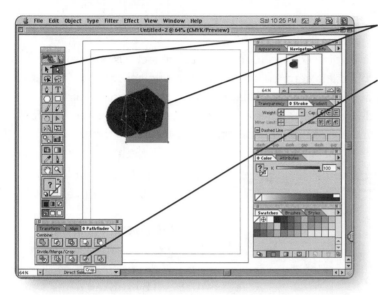

1. Select all of the **objects** with the Lasso or Selection tool.

2. Click on **Crop** in the Pathfinder palette. The objects will be cropped to conform to the shape of the front-most object, but use the colors of the rearward objects as the fill.

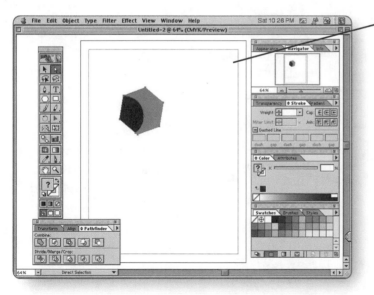

3. Command+click on an empty place on the artboard. The object will be deselected, and the cropping will be completed.

Using the Outline Tool

The Outline command removes the object fills and creates stroked line segments to define the original objects. The lines around the objects will be the color of the original fill. The individual line segments are split wherever they intersect. To start, revert the three objects to their original form.

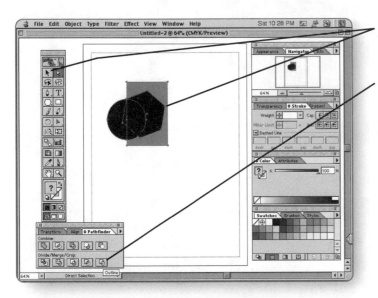

1. Select all of the **objects** with the Selection or Lasso tool.

2. Click on **Outline** in the Pathfinder palette. The object fills will disappear and be replaced by stroked paths defining the borders of the objects.

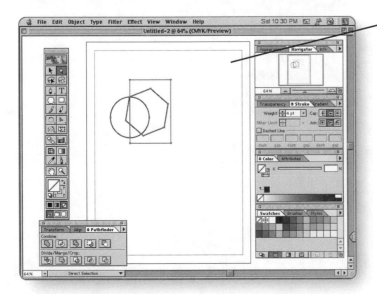

3. Command+click on an **empty place** on the artboard. The object will be deselected.

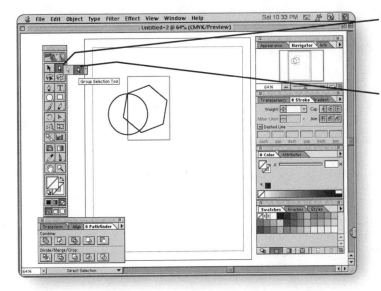

4. Click and hold on the **Direct Selection tool**. A pop-up palette will appear.

5. Point to the **Group Selection tool** and release the mouse button. The tool will become active.

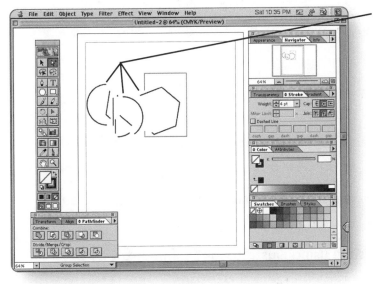

6. Click and drag on any **path section**. The path sections will move to the desired location.

Part II Review Questions

1. What sorts of shapes can you create with Illustrator's Preset Shape tools? *See "Using the Preset Shape Tools" in Chapter 3*

2. In which palette is the spiral tool located? *See "Drawing a Spiral" in Chapter 3*

3. Which tool would you use to draw a free-form shape? *See "Drawing Freeform Objects" in Chapter 3*

4. What is the maximum number of actions that can be undone using the Undo command? *See " Moving an Object" in Chapter 4*

5. How do move an object when you want to change its position onscreen? *See "Moving an Object" in Chapter 4*

6. Which tool do you use to resize an object? *See "Resizing an Object" in Chapter 5*

7. What is the shear tool used for? *See "Shearing an Object" in Chapter 5*

8. What tool produces an effect like "graph paper for the screen"? *See "Displaying the Grid" in Chapter 6*

9. Which tool would you use to make a perfectly rounded circle? *See "Working with Paths and Pathfinders" in chapter 7*

10. What actions are possible using Illustrator's Pathfinder tools? *See "Working with Paths and Pathfinders" in Chapter 7*

PART III

Working with Objects and Text

8

Using Color, Strokes and Fills

More often than not, you're going to want to get some color into your artwork. You know there are two basic parts to every object. The first part is the path of the object that creates its boundary (the *stroke*), and the second is the area inside that boundary (the *fill*). Now let's get down to the nitty-gritty of how to stroke your paths and instill those big open inside areas of your objects with just the right color, gradient, or pattern fill. In this chapter you'll learn how to…

- Work with strokes and fills
- Use patterns, transparencies, and gradients
- Mix your own custom colors
- Work with the Swatches palette
- Use the Paint Bucket and Eyedropper tools

Dashing Off a Few Lines

Inside the Stroke palette, you'll find the tools to create dashed or dotted lines. When you use these tools with different line weights and endcaps, you can come up with an endless variety of effects. Draw a simple shape and give it a line weight of about six or seven points.

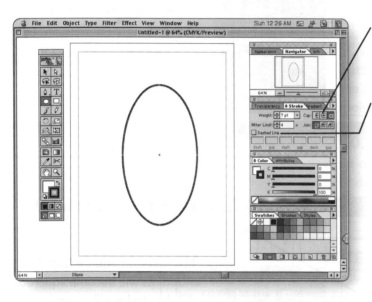

1. Click on **Rounded Cap**. The Round Cap box will be selected.

2. Click on the **Dashed Line check box** to select it. The line will become a dashed line according to the attributes you'll enter next in the Dash and Gap boxes.

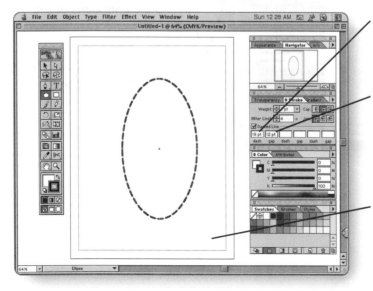

3. Double-click in the first **dash text box** and **enter** a **dash value**.

4. Double-click in the first **gap text box, enter** a **gap value,** and press **Enter**. The line dashes and gaps will be applied accordingly.

5. Point away from the object and **Command+click** to deselect.

The Swatches Palette

When you're "coloring inside the lines" with Illustrator, you are working with fills. A *fill* can be a solid color, a gradient, or a pattern. You can find examples of each of these fills stored on the Swatches palette.

No-Frills Fills: Solid Colors

To get a feel for working with the Swatches palette, let's start by applying a solid color fill. Create another object to fill and leave it selected.

1. Click on **Fill** on the toolbox. The Fill box will move to the front of the toolbox. Any treatment you select next will be applied to the object's fill, not the stroke.

2. Click on the **Swatches tab**. The Swatches palette will move to the front.

3. Click on **Show All Swatches** at the bottom of the Swatches palette. All of the default swatches will be visible.

4. Click on a **solid-color swatch**. The color will be applied to the selected fill.

5. Command+click on an **empty place** on the artboard. The object will be deselected.

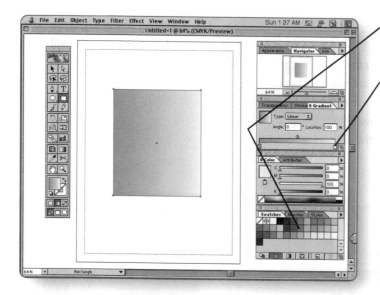

6. Click and hold on a color swatch in the Swatches palette.

7. Drag the color swatch over the other Gradient slider and release the mouse button. The slider will become the new color, and the representative color will change in the rectangle.

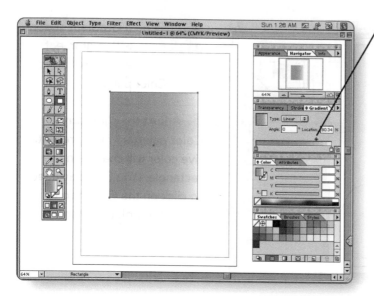

8. Click and drag the slider diamond on top of the Gradient bar. The percentage of each color on either side of the diamond slider will change accordingly.

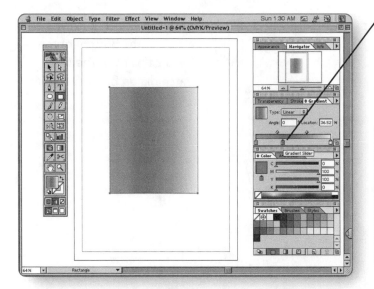

9. Click anywhere below the Gradient bar. A new color slider will appear. Re-color it with any of the methods you learned previously.

TIP

A new slider button will appear with every new color slider you create. Drag the new button to adjust to desired setting.

Saving Your Gradient as a Swatch

If you've created a gradient you really like or plan to use often, you can add it to the Swatches palette and even give it a name. When you have your gradient fill exactly as you want it, follow these steps.

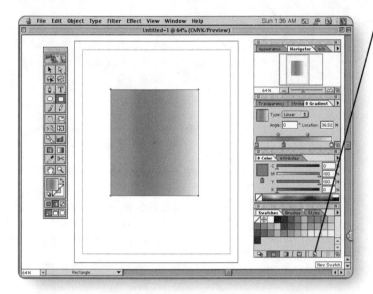

1. Option+click on **New Swatch** at the bottom of the Swatches palette. The New Swatch dialog box will appear.

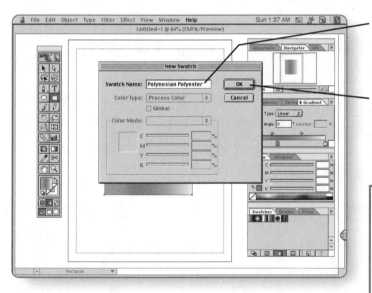

2. Enter a **name** for your new gradient fill in the Swatch Name text box.

3. Click on **OK**. The dialog box will close and the new swatch will appear on the Swatches palette.

TIP

You also can use the drag-and-drop method for creating swatches, as you learned earlier in this chapter.

Double-click on the new swatch to open the Name dialog box, in which you can give the swatch a more descriptive name.

Linear versus Radial Gradients

The gradient we've been working with is a linear gradient. The color blends in a *linear* gradient go from one side to the other as bands of color. A *radial* gradient, on the other hand, blends the colors out from a middle area like a sunburst. You can change a radial gradient to a linear gradient or vice versa. Select the object from the preceding exercise with the Selection or Lasso tool.

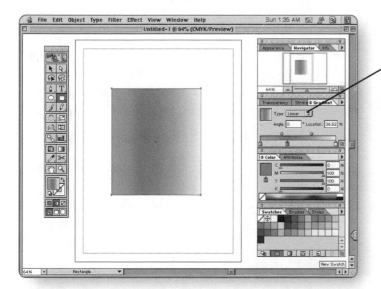

1. Click and hold on the Linear/Radial pop-up menu. The menu will appear.

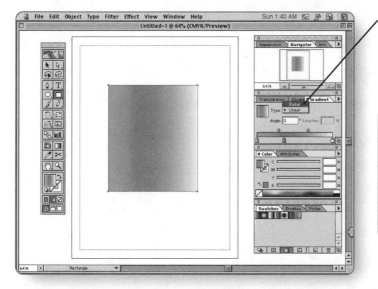

2. Point to the option you want and release the mouse button. The gradient will change to the selected type.

NOTE

The color on the left of the Gradient bar will be the center color in a radial gradient.

Tweaking with the Gradient Tool

If you thought you might be limited to dead-center or straight-line gradient fills, think again. To give you more artistic freedom, Illustrator includes the Gradient tool, so you can adjust the direction and spread of a linear gradient or relocate the center of a radial gradient. Select an object with a radial gradient to follow these steps.

Changing a Radial Center Location

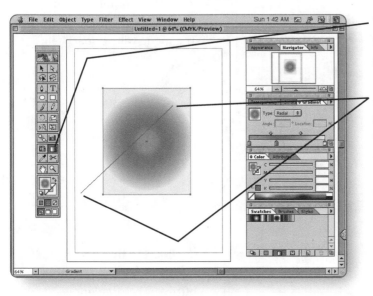

1. **Click** on the **Gradient tool** in the toolbox. The tool will become active.

2. **Click and drag** over **the spot** where you want to place the new center of the radial gradient. (The new center does not have to be inside the object.)

Changing the Direction of a Linear Gradient

You can adjust a linear gradient similarly. To prepare for the next steps, use the Linear/Radial option box in the Gradient palette to change the gradient back to linear, and select it with the Selection tool.

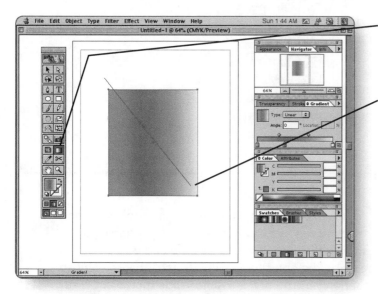

1. Click on the **Gradient tool**. The Gradient tool will become active.

2. Click near the **lower right corner** of the rectangle and **drag** to near the **upper left corner** of the rectangle.

3. Release the **mouse button**. The direction of the gradient will be a right-to-left diagonal through the rectangle.

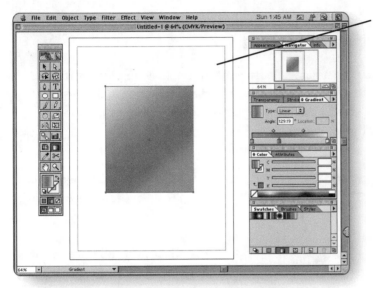

4. **Command+click** on an empty place on the artboard. The object will be deselected, and your new gradient will be implemented.

TIP

As you experiment with the Gradient tool, you'll find that you can "squeeze" the colors by dragging a shorter distance. If you begin and end your drag outside the object, you will "stretch" the gradient so that only a little of it is visible inside the object. Like everything else in this program, the more you play, the better you get.

Another Fine Mesh! Introducing the Gradient Mesh Tool

The Gradient Mesh tool allows you to place several gradients onto the same object and edit them in much the same way that you would edit a path. Using this option, you can create very realistic, three-dimensional surfaces on objects with variable smooth transitions in colors, shadows, and highlights.

For the exercises in this section, start with an object like the
heart shape in my illustration, give it a solid fill, and select it
with the Selection tool.

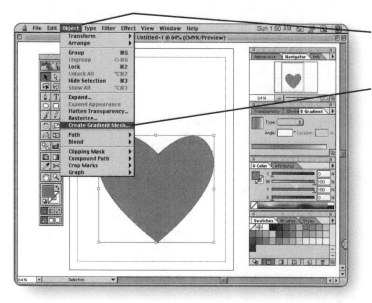

1. **Click** on **Object**. The Object
menu will open.

2. **Click** on **Create Gradient
Mesh**. The Gradient Mesh
dialog box will appear.

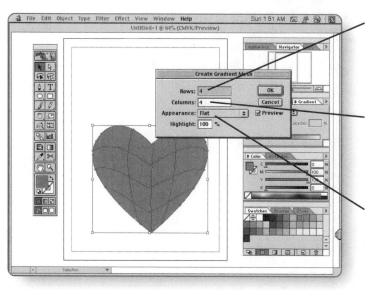

3. **Double-click** in the **Rows
text box** and **type** the **number**
of horizontal rows you want in
the mesh.

4. **Double-click** in the
Columns text box and **type** the
number of vertical columns you
want in the mesh.

5. **Select** a **pattern type** from
the Appearance pop-up menu.
(In this example, I chose Flat.)

NOTE

The Appearance pop-up menu gives you three choices:

• **Flat** maintains the solid-color appearance on the object.

• **To Center** puts a highlight in the center of the object.

• **To Edge** places a highlight around the object's edge.

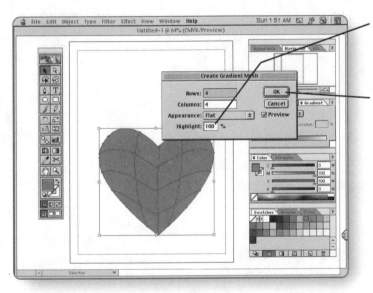

6. Double-click in the Highlight text box and type a percentage to highlight.

7. Click on OK. The dialog box will close and the gradient mesh will appear on the object.

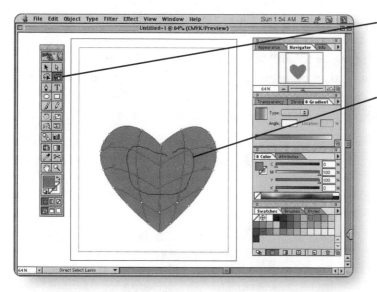

8. **Click** on the **Direct Lasso** tool. The Direct Lasso tool becomes active.

9. **Click and drag** around the **center portion** of the object and **release** the **mouse button**. (Or press Shift+click with the Direct Selection tool.) Some of the centermost mesh points are selected.

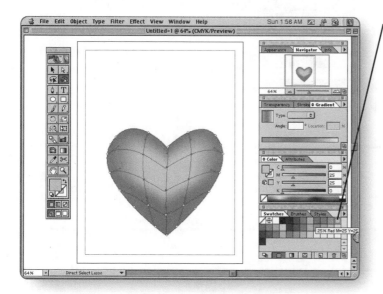

10. **Click** on a **color swatch** that is lighter than the original color of the object. The selected mesh points become the color of the new swatch, which creates a highlight on the object.

Leave everything as-is for the next exercise.

Creating New Mesh Points

With the Gradient Mesh tool, you can add as many new mesh points to an object as you need, so that you can fine-tune and add more detail to your surface gradients. Select the object from the preceding exercise and follow these steps.

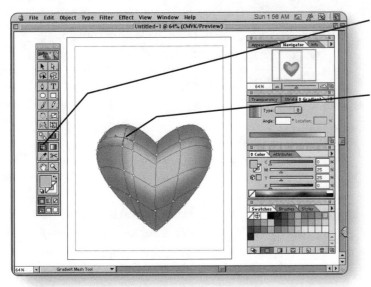

1. **Click** on the **Gradient Mesh tool.** The tool will become active.

2. **Click** on the **location** inside the object where you want to place a new mesh point. A new selected mesh point will placed with corresponding vertical and horizontal mesh lines.

NOTE

The new mesh point will be assigned whatever color is currently in the Fill box.

TIP

To delete a mesh point, hold down the Option key and click on the unwanted point with the Gradient Mesh tool.

Tweaking Mesh Points

You can move and stretch the mesh points the same way that you reshape a path. Doing so allows you to control the shape and size of the gradient in the immediate area.

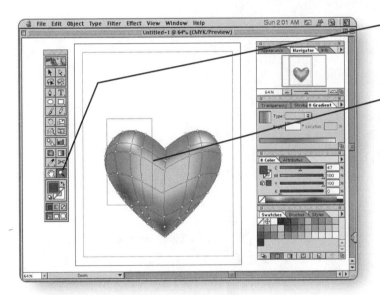

1. **Click** on the **Zoom** in the toolbox. The tool will become active.

2. **Drag** a **marquee** around the area to be magnified.

3. **Release** the **mouse button**. The area will be magnified onscreen.

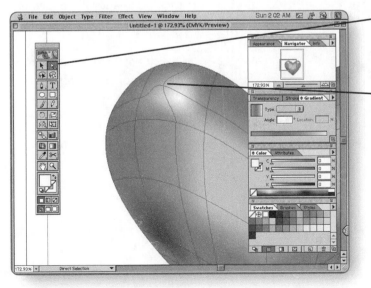

4. **Click** on the **Direct Selection** tool in the toolbox. The tool will become active.

5. **Click and hold** on a **mesh point** and **drag it** to a new position; then **release** the **mouse button**. The mesh point and the center of its gradient will be relocated.

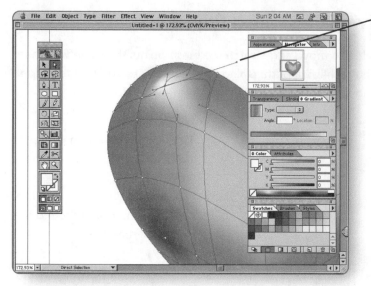

6. **Click and drag** on the **mesh point path lines**. The mesh will warp accordingly, pulling and thinning the gradient in the direction of the warp.

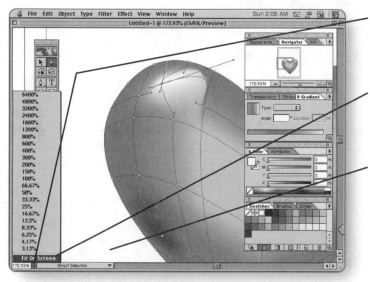

7. **Click** on the **Zoom down arrow**. A pop-up menu will appear.

8. **Click** on **Fit On Screen**. The magnified image will reduce to fit the screen.

9. **Click anywhere** in an empty spot to deselect the object.

Dragging the Patch

One more way to edit the gradient mesh is to move a mesh patch. A *mesh patch* is the shape created inside the boundaries of any four intersecting mesh lines. You can use the Direct Selection tool to move the patches around in chunks.

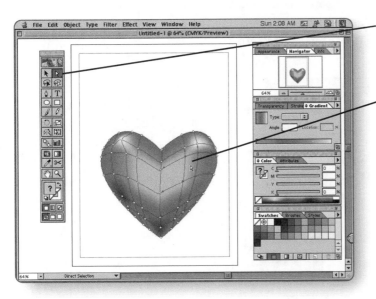

1. **Click** on the **Direct Selection tool**. The tool will become active.

2. **Click and hold** inside a **mesh patch area**. The four points on the corners of the patch will be selected.

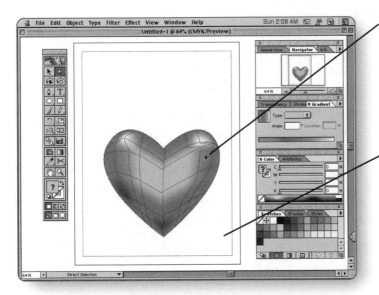

3. **Drag** the **patch** to a new location and **release** the **mouse button**. The patch will be moved and the corresponding mesh lines and gradients will change accordingly.

4. **Click** on an **empty place** on the artboard. The object will be deselected, and your snazzy new gradient will be implemented.

Creating a Fill Pattern

Okay, if you think gradient fills are cool, wait until you try a pattern! Patterns are a lot of fun to play with—it's sort of like designing a quilt or wallpaper. You can use literally anything you draw as a pattern, as long as it doesn't have a gradient, another pattern, or an EPS file. You can apply a pattern as a fill or a stroke, but you may need to give the stroke a lot of weight to do the pattern justice.

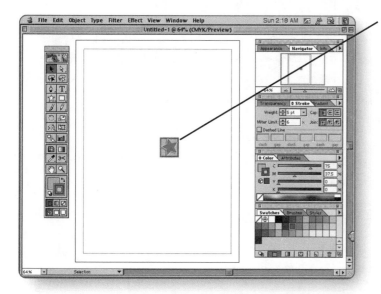

To perform the steps in this section, you'll need to start with a small object or drawing to serve as the basis of your pattern. I chose a small red star shape surrounded by a purple square.

CAUTION

Try not to get too elaborate with your pattern designs. Because of the memory required to process a complex, repetitive pattern, you can very easily overload your average printer's processing capabilities. (And if your pattern is that complex, it's likely too intricate to make a good-looking pattern anyway. Remember, with special effects, a little goes a very long way.)

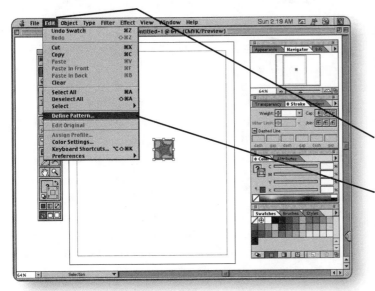

1. **Select** the **entire drawing** with the Selection or Lasso tool. (Or press Command+A for Select All). The drawing will be selected.

2. **Click** on **Edit**. The Edit menu will open.

3. **Click** on **Define Pattern**. The menu will close and the New Swatch dialog box will appear.

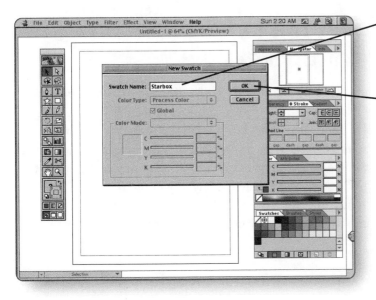

4. **Enter** a **name** for your pattern in the Swatch Name text box.

5. **Click** on **OK**. The dialog box will close and the new swatch will be placed in the Swatches palette.

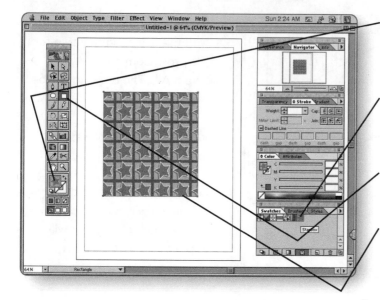

6. **Click** on the **Fill box**. The Fill box will move to the front of the toolbox.

7. **Click** on the **new swatch** to select it. The swatch will appear in the Fill box.

8. **Click** on a **shape tool**. The tool will become active.

9. **Drag** a **shape**. The shape will be filled with your new pattern.

Using the Eyedropper and Paint Bucket

While we're on the subject of fills and strokes, you'll definitely want to know about the Eyedropper and Paint Bucket tools. These handy little guys are a big help! Using the Eyedropper tool, you can slurp up a sample of the attributes of one object and immediately drop them onto another object. Similarly, the Paint Bucket tool quickly fills any object on the screen with the currently selected stroke and fill. To practice these techniques, create two objects with different strokes and fills.

Sampling with the Eyedropper

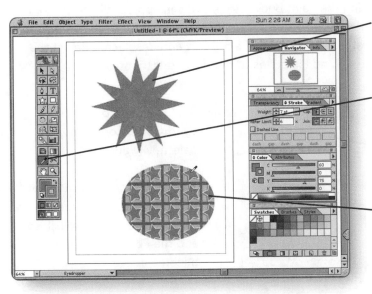

1. **Select** an **object** in your drawing using the Selection tool.

2. **Click** on the **Eyedropper tool** in the toolbox. The tool will become active, and the pointer will change to resemble an eyedropper.

3. **Click** on the **unselected object**. The selected object will change to take on the fill and stroke of the object sampled by the Eyedropper.

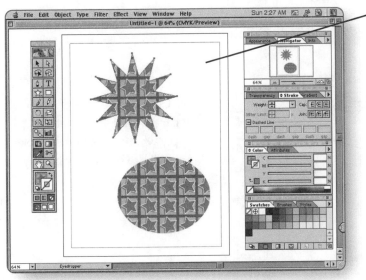

4. **Command+click** on an **empty place** on the artboard. The object will be deselected, and your snazzy new gradient will be implemented.

Filling with the Paint Bucket

Using the Paint Bucket tool, you can apply a fill and stroke in one fell swoop (or at least in one simple click). To see how this tool works, first create an object and deselect it. Preset the Stroke and Fill boxes to the desired attributes.

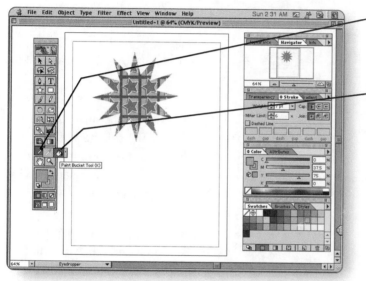

1. Click and hold on the Eyedropper tool. A pop-up palette will appear.

2. Point to the Paint Bucket tool and release the mouse button. The palette will close and the Paint Bucket will become active.

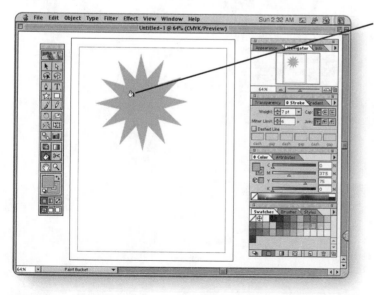

3. Click on the object. Illustrator will immediately apply whatever is in the Stroke and Fill boxes to the object you indicated.

Preview and Outline Views

There are times when you might just want (or need) to look at the bare bones of your artwork. The outline view eliminates all of the fills and strokes to allow you to do just that.

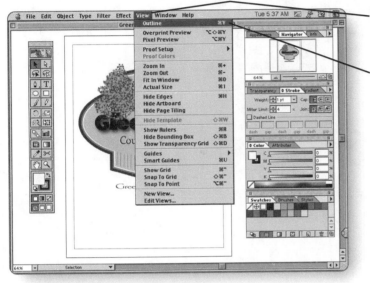

1. **Click** on **View**. The View menu will open.

2. **Click** on **Outline**. The menu will close and the artwork will change to the Outline mode.

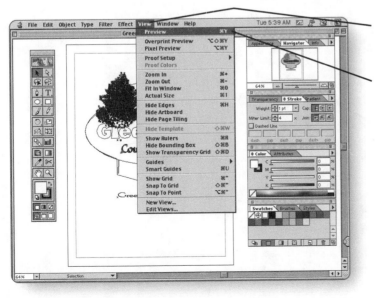

3. **Click** on **View**. The View menu will open.

4. **Click** on **Preview**.

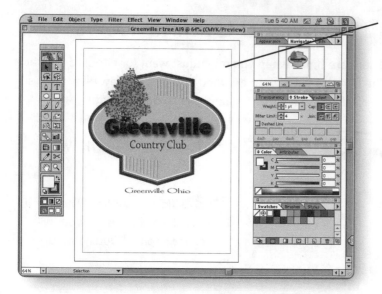

The menu will close and the Preview (color) mode will be restored.

9

Using the Paintbrush

The Paintbrush is the first tool that usually comes to mind when thinking about art. This chapter is not so much about the Paintbrush tool itself as it is about the brush strokes you create with it. The brushes in Illustrator fall into four categories: Calligraphy brush, Scatter brush, Art brush, and Pattern brush. These brushes offer the digital artist much more than just a way to spread color onto the page. In this chapter, you will learn how to …

- Select and use the Paintbrush tool
- Open and explore the Brushes palette
- Apply a brush stroke to a path
- Create examples of new brushes
- Open brush libraries

Introducing the Paintbrush Tool

The Paintbrush tool works much the same as the Pencil tool, in that you click and drag to create a line. The difference is in the kind of line you create. When you click on the Paintbrush tool, a brush stroke is selected from the default brushes in the Brushes palette. Think of the Paintbrush as a way to stroke a path on-the-fly with anything you can imagine—from a calligraphic swash, to a decorative border, to a swarm of bumblebees. Let's activate the Paintbrush tool and the Brushes palette and look at some examples of each brush.

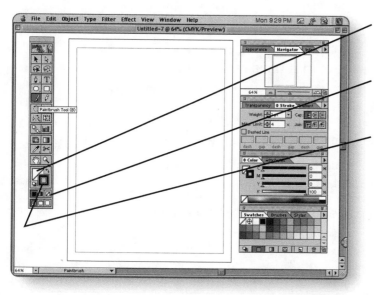

1. **Click** on the **Fill box**. The Fill box will come to the front.

2. **Click** on **None**. The Fill box will show no fill.

3. **Click** on the **Stroke box**. The Stroke box will come forward.

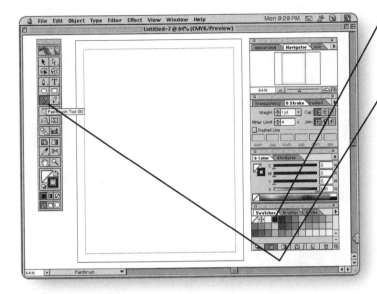

4. **Click** the **Black swatch** in the Swatches palette. The stroke selection will be black.

5. **Click** on the **Paintbrush tool.** The tool will become active.

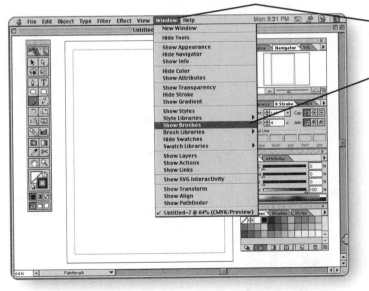

6. **Click** on **Window.** The Window menu will open.

7. **Point** to **Show Brushes** and **release** the **mouse button.**

TIP

As a shortcut replacement for steps 6 and 7, just click on the Brushes tab (if the palette is visible). The Brushes palette will appear with the default stroke selection.

Applying a Calligraphy Stroke

Use these brushes to create calligraphic writing and dramatic swashes.

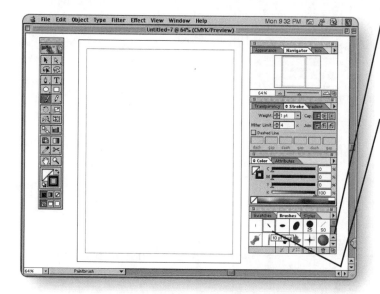

1. **Click and hold** on the **scroll-up arrow** on the Brushes pallet (if necessary) until the top row of brushes is visible.

2. **Click** on a **Calligraphy brush** in the top row. The brush will become active.

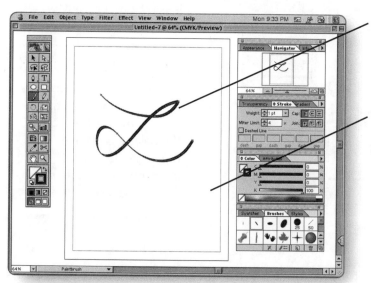

3. **Drag** a **path** with the Paintbrush tool. A calligraphic paint stroke will be applied to the line path.

4. **Command+click** on an **empty place** on the artboard. The object will be deselected.

Applying a Scatter Stroke

Use these brushes to scatter small shapes, pictures, or icons along the path. You can do some pretty amazing stuff with scatter strokes!

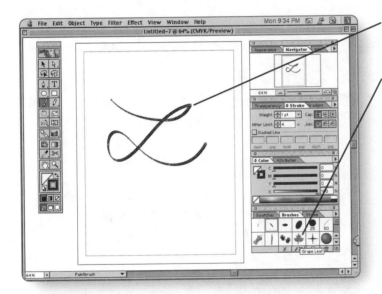

1. Select the **object** from the preceding example.

2. Click on a **Scatter brush** in the second row of the Brushes palette. The Scatter brush stroke will be applied to the path.

3. Command+click on an **empty place** on the artboard. The object will be deselected.

Applying an Art Stroke

Like the Scatter brushes, Art brushes will work with small images. But instead of scattering several images along the path, the Art brush stretches a single image along the length of the path.

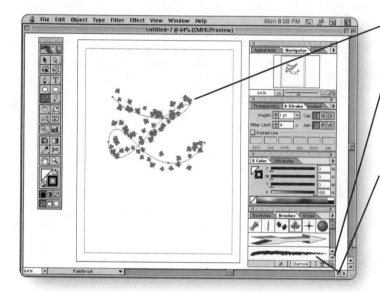

1. **Select** the **object** from the preceding example.

2. **Click and hold** on the **scroll-down arrow** in the Brushes palette (if necessary). The Art brushes will scroll into view.

3. **Click** on an **Art brush.** The stroke will be applied to the selected path.

NOTE

Some of the Scatter or Art brushes will not produce the same color when applied that they appear to produce when viewed in the palette. You can change the color of these brushes by selecting the path that the brush stroke is applied to, and then changing the stroke color via the Stroke box in the toolbox. Remember, these brushes are strokes, not fills.

Applying a Pattern Stroke

You can apply a Pattern brush to any stroke. Depending on the pattern, this stroke might look fine on our big scripted capital L, for instance. But a Pattern brush stroke really comes into its own when it's used as a decorative border around a geometric shape.

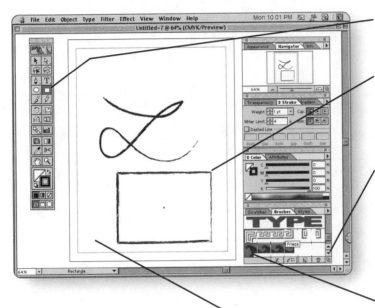

1. **Click** on the **Rectangle tool**. The tool will become active.

2. **Draw** a **rectangle**. A rectangle will appear with the most recently used brush applied to the stroke.

3. **Click** and **hold** on the **scroll-down button** on the Brushes palette until the Pattern brushes appear. (The Pattern brushes are broken up into segments on the palette.)

4. **Click** on a **pattern brush**. The selected brush will be applied to the stroke of the rectangle.

5. **Command+click** on an **empty place** on the artboard. The object will be deselected.

Applying a New Stroke Weight

You can change the weight of a brush stroke the same way you change the weight of any other stroke—by using the Stroke palette. To get started, reselect the rectangle from the previous section and click on the Stroke palette tab to bring it forward (if necessary).

1. Click on the **Weight down arrow**. The stroke weight submenu will open.

2. Point to the **desired stroke weight** and **release** the **mouse button**. The new stroke weight will be applied to the selected stroke.

3. Command+click on an empty place on the artboard. The object will be deselected.

Creating Your Own Brushes

Now that you've seen what the brushes can do, you will naturally want to try to build a few brushes of your own. To do so, you need to open one of the four Brush option dialog boxes and tell Illustrator how to customize your brushes.

Creating a Calligraphy Brush

For those times when you want to express yourself with your very own version of the quill pen, or maybe design one of those swashbuckling romance novel cover titles, Illustrator gives you the ability to make your own calligraphy pens and brushes.

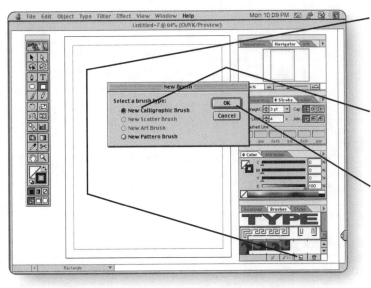

1. **Click** on the **New Brush icon** on the bottom of the Brushes palette. The New Brush dialog box will appear.

2. **Click** on the **New Calligraphic Brush button**. The button will be selected.

3. **Click** on **OK**. The Calligraphic Brush Options dialog box will appear.

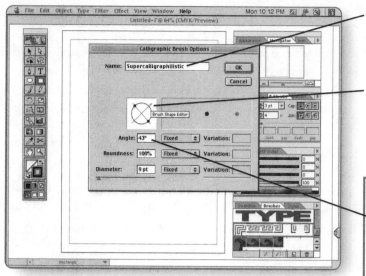

4. **Enter** a **new name** for the brush. (In the sample, I called it SuperCalligraphillistic).

5. **Click and drag** on the **arrowhead** in the Brush Shape Editor box. The brush will rotate to the desired angle.

TIP

Alternatively, type a specific value in the Angle text box.

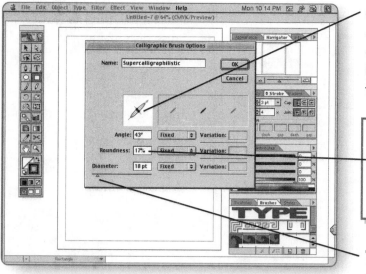

6. **Click and drag inward** on one of the black dots on the circle in the Brush Shape Editor box. The shape of the brush will flatten accordingly.

TIP

Alternatively, type a specific value in the Roundness text box.

7. **Drag** the **Diameter slider** (or type a value in the Diameter text box). The size of the brush will change.

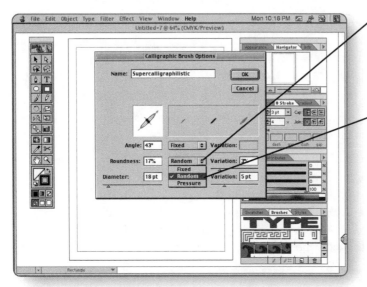

8. Click on the **pop-up menu** to the right of the Roundness text box. The pop-up menu will appear.

9. Click on **Fixed**, **Random**, or **Pressure**. Your choice will be selected.

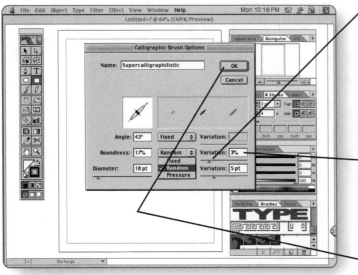

10. Drag the **Variation slider** (if Fixed is not selected). The variation size or percentage values will appear in the Variation text box.

TIP

Alternatively, type a specific value in the Variation text box.

---

11. Click on **OK**. The dialog box will close and the new brush icon will appear in the Brushes palette window.

NOTE

For each of the brush settings, you can choose the following options, depending on the effect you're going for:

• **Fixed** will lock the specified value throughout the brush stroke.

• **Random** will cause Illustrator to change the value settings randomly between the selected variables of the brush stroke.

• **Pressure** will react to a pressure-sensitive tablet.

You can see how the changes you make to the settings affect the brush by observing the dots in the window at the right of the Brush Shape Editor. The black dot in the middle represents the brush angle, roundness, and diameter as specified in the text boxes. The two gray dots represent the extremes of the Variation settings.

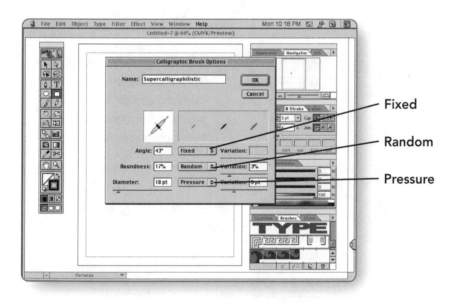

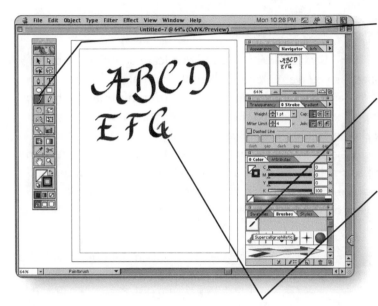

12. Click on the **Paintbrush tool**. The tool will become active.

13. Click on the **new Calligraphy brush** in the Brushes palette. It will be selected.

14. Click and drag on the **artboard**. The new brush will be applied to the strokes.

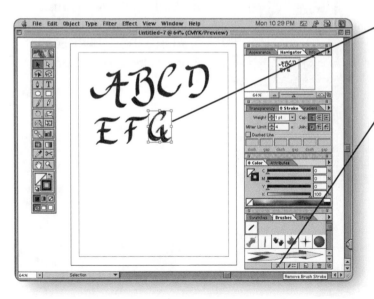

15. If you want to remove a brush stroke from any path, **select** the **path** by clicking and dragging over the object.

16. Click on the **Remove Brush Stroke icon** at the bottom of the Brushes palette. The brush stroke will be removed.

Creating a Scatter Brush

With the Scatter brush, you can duplicate an object as many times as you want along the length of a path. Like the Calligraphy brush, the Scatter brush uses information that you supply in a dialog box. But before that happens, you have to make an image for the Scatter brush to scatter. I've made a picture of a pine tree, but anything will do. It doesn't have to be as small as I've made this one, either—you can determine the size of the object in the dialog box. So draw or place an object on the artboard and then follow these steps.

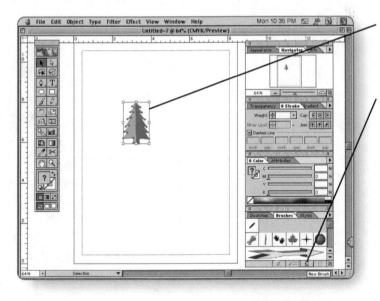

1. **Click** on the **object** with the Selection tool. The object will be selected.

2. **Click** on the **New Brush icon** on the bottom of the Brushes palette. The New Brush dialog box will appear.

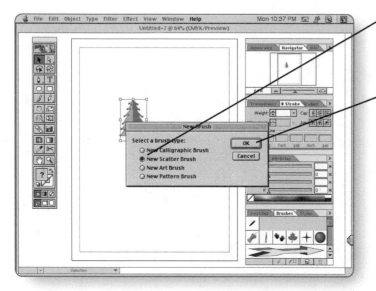

3. Click on the **New Scatter Brush button**. It will be selected.

4. Click on **OK**. The Scatter Brush Options dialog box will appear.

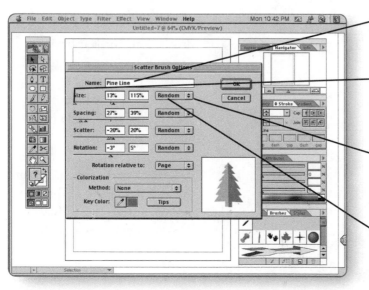

5. Enter a **name** for the new Scatter brush.

6. Click on the **Size slider** and drag it to the left. The size percentage will be reduced.

7. Click on the **Size settings pop-up menu**. The menu will appear.

8. Click on **Random**. A second, black slider will appear below the Size slider bar.

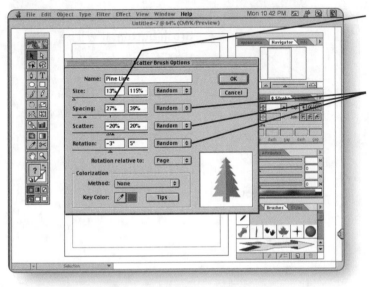

9. **Click and drag** the **new slider** (if desired). The other size variance will be changed.

10. **Repeat steps 6-9** to change the variance percentages of Spacing, Scatter, and Rotation.

11. **Click** on **OK**. The dialog box will close and the new Scatter brush icon will appear on the Brushes palette.

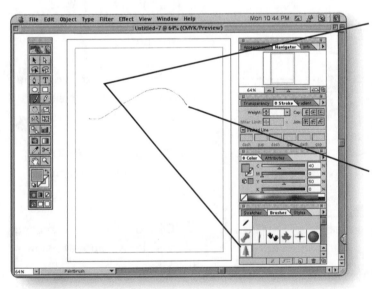

12. **Click** on the **New Scatter Brush icon**. The brush will be selected.

13. **Click** on the **Paintbrush tool**. The tool will become active.

14. **Click and drag** a **path** on the artboard. Release the mouse button. The path will be stroked with the new Scatter brush.

Exercising Your Options

How about that! With one stroke of the Paintbrush, we've created an Alpine forest. But if it isn't exactly to your liking, you can make changes and tweak the brush stroke until it's the way you want it.

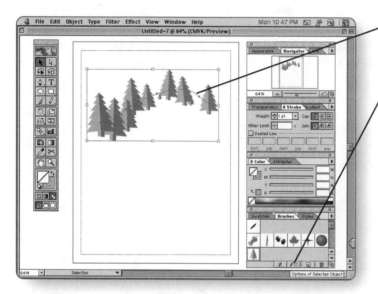

1. **Select** the **path** with the Selection tool. The path will be selected.

2. **Click** on the **Options of Selected Object icon** at the bottom of the Brushes palette. The Stroke Options (Scatter Brush) dialog box will appear.

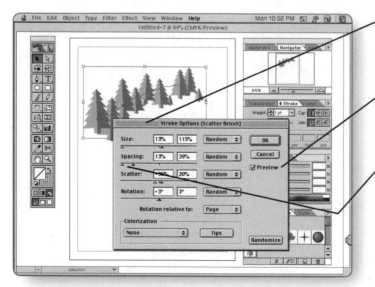

3. **Click and drag** the **dialog box title bar** (if needed) to make the artwork visible.

4. **Click** on the **Preview check box** (if it isn't checked). The Preview box will be checked.

5. **Make** any necessary changes with the sliders and drop-down selections.

6. **Click** on **OK**. The dialog box will close and the stroke will reflect any changes.

Creating an Art Brush

With the Art brush, you are stroking a path with a premade piece of art; but unlike the Scatter brush, the single object stretches and warps along the path instead of multiplying and scattering. With practice, you can use this brush to imitate chalks, pastels, graphite, or any number of art supplies. You can also create pictures or words and bend, twist, and distort them along a line. The Art brush can make a brush out of almost anything. So create or place a piece of art on the artboard.

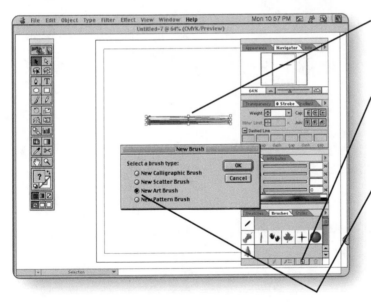

1. Click on the **object** with the Selection tool. The object will be selected.

2. Click on the **New Brush icon** at the bottom of the Brushes palette. The New Brush dialog box will appear.

3. Click on the **New Art Brush button**. The button will be selected.

4. Click on **OK**. The Art Brush Options dialog box will appear.

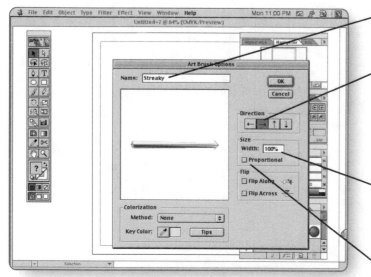

5. Enter a **name** for the new Art brush.

6. Click on a **Direction box** to establish the direction the stroke will take in relation to the object. The Direction box will be selected.

7. Double-click in the **Width text box** and enter a **width percentage value**.

8. Click on the **Proportional check box** if you want the object's proportions to be preserved.

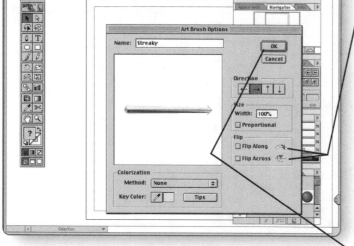

9. Click on one or both of the **Flip boxes** if you want the object to flip along or across the path.

NOTE

Flip Along will reverse the object from left to right along the length of the path. **Flip Across** will reverse the object up and down across the path line.

---

10. Click on **OK**. The dialog box will close and the new Art brush will appear on the brushes palette.

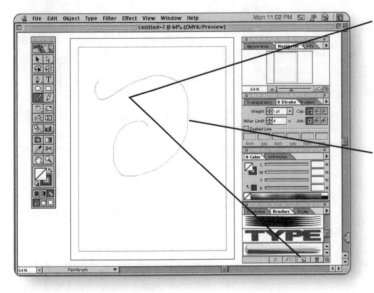

11. Click on the **New Art Brush icon**. It will be selected.

12. Click on the **Paintbrush tool**. The tool will become active.

13. Click and drag a **path** with the Paintbrush. A dotted line will appear.

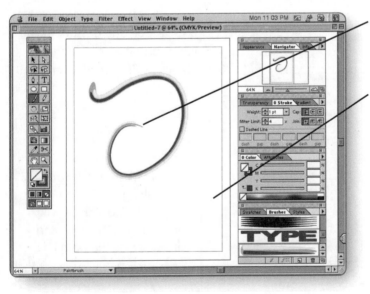

14. Release the **mouse button**. The path will be stroked with the new Art brush.

15. Command+click on an **empty place** on the artboard. The object will be deselected.

Creating a Pattern Brush

Remember when we made patterns to use as fills? Well, guess what? You can use those patterns (or any other pattern) to create a Pattern brush. The Pattern brush is really a different animal, and to build a good one takes a little planning. It's sort of like visualizing a jigsaw puzzle and then creating the pieces to put it together. Once you get the hang of it, it can be a lot of fun!

Making Pattern Brush Tiles

Pattern brushes are made up of individual square patterns or *tiles*. You will need to make side, corner, and end tiles to create a complete Pattern brush. The trick is to place the tiles so that they interact with each other to create a smooth, continuous design along a path.

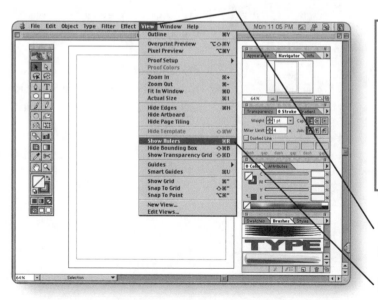

TIP

Although it really isn't required, it can be helpful to turn on the Show Grid and the Snap To Grid options when you're creating new tiles for the Pattern brush.

---

1. Click on **View**. The View menu will open.

2. Click on **Show Rulers**. The menu will close and the rulers will appear at the top and side of the work area.

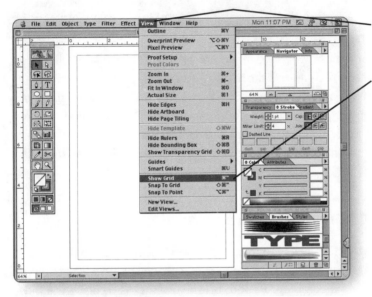

3. Click on **View**. The View menu will open.

4. Click on **Show Grid**. The menu will close and a grid will cover the work area.

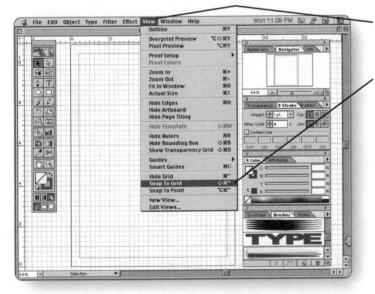

5. Click on **View**. The View menu will open.

6. Click on **Snap To Grid**. The menu will close and the Snap To Grid option will become active.

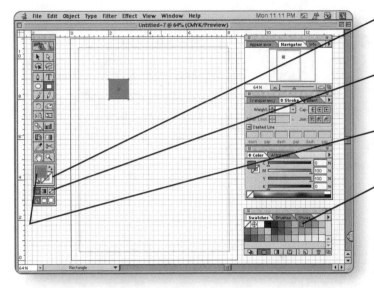

7. Click on the **Stroke box**. It will move forward.

8. Click on **None**. The path will receive no stroke.

9. Click on the **Fill box**. It will move forward.

10. Click on a **solid-color swatch**. The fill will receive the color you selected.

11. Click on the **Rectangle tool**. The Rectangle tool will be active.

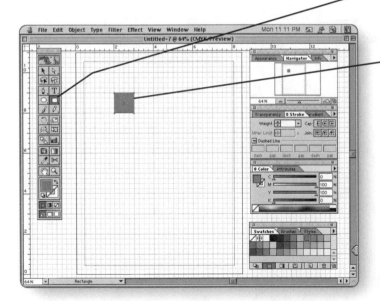

12. Click and drag a **one-inch square tile**. A selected tile will appear on the artboard. Do not deselect it.

NOTE

A tile does not necessarily have to be a filled square. As a matter of fact, it doesn't have to be a square at all. I'm just using this as an example. A tile is easier to visualize if you use a square as a background guideline. You can always give it a fill of None before you turn it into a pattern.

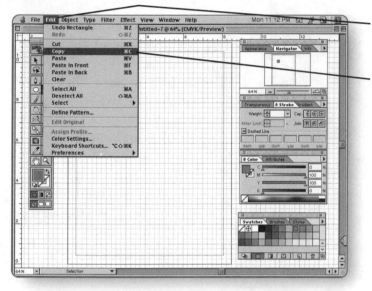

13. Click on **Edit**. The Edit menu will open.

14. Click on **Copy**. The menu will close and a copy of the tile will be placed in the Clipboard.

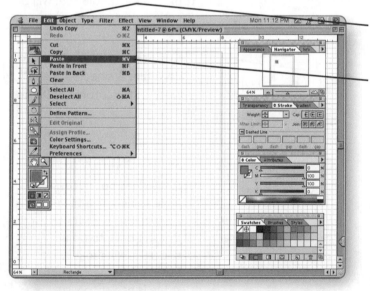

15. Click on **Edit**. The Edit menu will open.

16. Click on **Paste**. The menu will close and the copy of the tile will be pasted on the artboard.

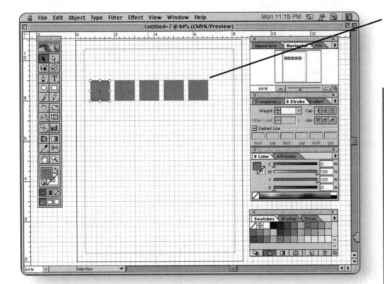

17. Repeat steps **15** and **16** until you have five tiles on the artboard.

TIP

You can use Command+C and Command+V as shortcuts for the Copy and Paste commands, respectively. Of course, skip steps 13-16 altogether and just click and drag the tile while holding down the Option key until you have cloned the tile five times.

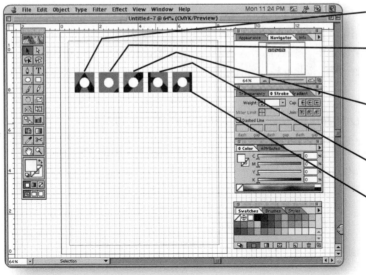

18. Design a **side tile**.

19. Design an **outer corner tile**.

20. Design an **inner corner tile**.

21. Design a **start tile**.

22. Design an **end tile**.

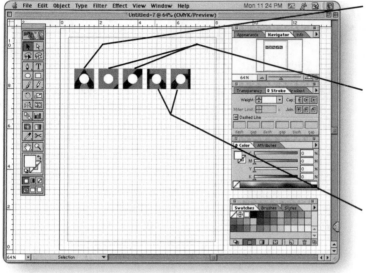

- A **side tile** is the one that will be repeated most often along the path, so you might think of it as a link in a chain.

- The **corner tiles** are needed only if you're creating something like a border around a rectangle—perhaps framing a picture, for example.

- The **start** and **end tiles** are applied to an open-ended path, like a Paintbrush stroke. The start tile is applied at the beginning of the stroke, and the end tile is applied at the end of the stroke. (Imagine that!)

It might help you to double-click one of the existing default Pattern brushes in the Brushes palette so that you can get into the dialog box and see how it was put together.

Turning the Tiles into Patterns

Now that you have the individual tiles for your pattern, it's time to create the pattern itself.

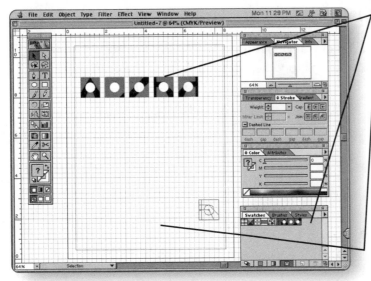

1. Click and drag a tile into the Swatches palette. A pattern swatch of the tile will appear in the Swatches palette.

2. Command+click on an empty place on the artboard. The object will be deselected.

3. Repeat steps 1-2 until all the tiles are turned into patterns.

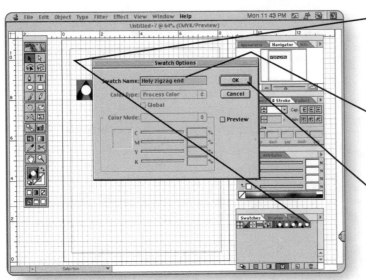

4. Double-click on one of the new Pattern swatches. The Swatch Options dialog box will appear.

5. Double-click in the Swatch Name text box and enter a name for the swatch.

6. Click on OK. The dialog box will close and the swatch will be named.

7. Repeat steps 3-6 with all five swatches.

NOTE

To help you keep track of the swatches, it's a good idea to add "side" to the side swatch name and "end" to the end swatch name.

Making the Pattern Brush

Now that you've designed the individual pieces, it's time to pull them all together and add them to the Brushes palette.

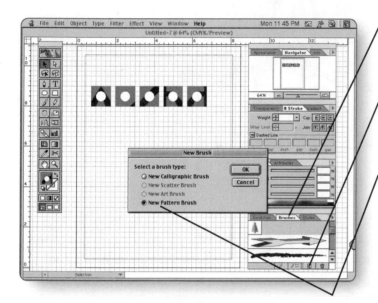

1. **Click** on the **Brushes tab**. The Brushes palette will move to the front.

2. **Click** the **New Brush icon**. The New Brush dialog box will appear.

3. **Click** on the **New Pattern Brush button**. It will be selected.

4. **Click** on **OK**. The Pattern Brush Options dialog box will appear.

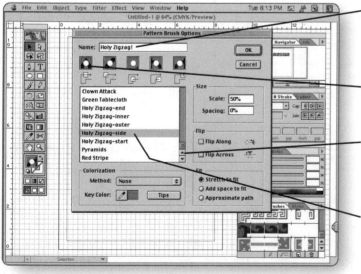

5. **Double-click** in the **Name text box** and **enter** a **name** for the brush.

6. **Click** on the **side tile window**. It will be selected.

7. **Click** on the **scroll arrows** (if needed). The name of the side tile will scroll into view.

8. **Click** on the **side tile name**. The side tile swatch will appear in the side tile window.

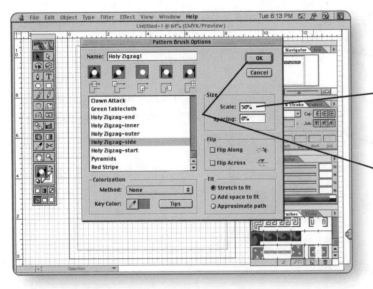

9. Repeat steps 6-8 until the windows all have the appropriate swatch showing.

10. Click on the **Scale text box** and **enter** a **width scale** for the brush (if desired).

11. Click on **OK**. The dialog box will close and the new Pattern brush tiles will appear on the Brushes palette.

NOTE

You will find that a lot of trial and error may be needed to make the brush do exactly what you want. But you can always edit the brush with the Options dialog box. (Click the second small icon at the bottom of the Brushes palette.)

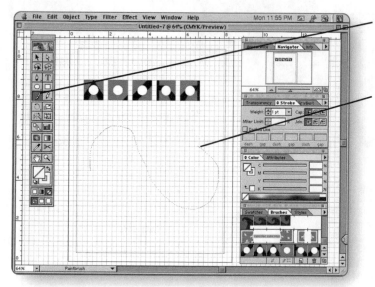

12. Click on the **Paintbrush tool**. The tool will become active.

13. Click and drag a **path**. A dotted line will appear.

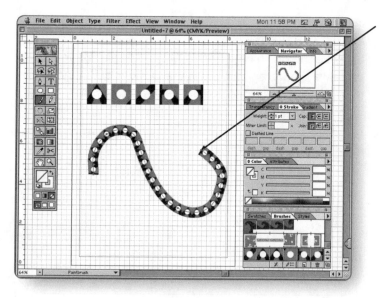

14. Release the **mouse button**. The path will be stroked with the new Pattern brush.

Getting into the Libraries

Well, now that you've gone to all of the trouble to learn to create your own brushes and patterns, you might as well know that you have about a zillion premade brushes right at your fingertips. If you did a complete installation of Illustrator, you probably have all these brushes on your hard drive. If not, they're on the Installation disc in the Illustrator Extras folder.

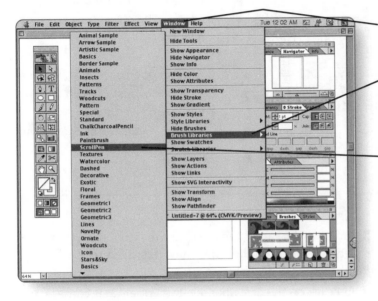

1. Click on **Window**. The Window menu will open.

2. Move the **pointer** to **Brush Libraries**. The Brush Libraries submenu will open.

3. Move the **pointer** over a brush category and **release** the **mouse button**. The menus will close, and the new Brushes palette will appear.

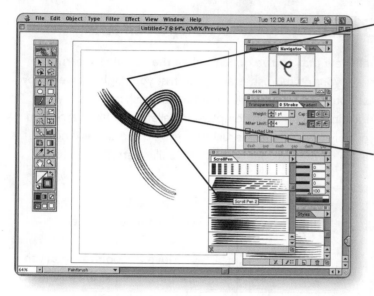

4. Click on a **brush** in the new palette. It will be selected.

5. Click on the **Paintbrush tool**. The tool will become active.

6. Click and drag a **path**, then **release** the **mouse button**. The path will be stroked with the new brush.

You can open as many brushes as you like. Just click on one of the brushes in the Library palette, and it will appear in the Brushes palette.

TIP

If you drag the tab of the new palette into the Brushes palette, it will place the whole new palette in the Brushes palette window.

If you click on the arrowhead in the upper right corner of the new palette, the palette menu will open. Click on Persistent to make that palette open every time you launch Illustrator

10

Filters, Effects, Appearances, and Styles

Photographers use filters to blur or soften an image, heighten particular colors, or distort a photo into an abstraction of wavy lines and blobs of color. In Illustrator, the Filters and Effects commands are used in much the same way.

Effects are very similar to filters, and you'll find that some of them seem to do exactly the same thing. The difference is that filters are permanent. They can be undone with the Undo command, but once they are placed, they're not editable. Effects, on the other hand, are compiled with all the other attributes of the object (fills, strokes, etc.) and are fully editable from within the Appearance palette.

The *Appearance* palette allows you to manage and edit all the enhancements in an object individually. You can experiment with an object to your heart's content without ever changing its basic shape.

A *style* is a saved appearance that you can keep in the Styles palette and apply to anything or everything you want just like a swatch or a brush. In this chapter, you'll learn …

- About filters and effects and how they're applied
- To use the Appearance palette
- To create and save styles

Filters

By my count, 26 Illustrator filters and 56 more Photoshop filters are included by default when you install Illustrator on your Mac. These filters are placed into groups on the Filter menu, with all the groups divided into submenus. Almost all these filters work through a dialog box. So, in the interest of keeping this book down to a portable weight, I'll list the filter groups and give a brief description of what they do. Then we'll apply one of the filters to an object as an example.

Group	Includes Filters that
Colors	Perform color editing, and blend and convert color modes.
Create	Create trim marks or mosaic tile effects.
Distort	Roughen, twirl, bloat, zigzag, stretch, and generally disfigure an object.
Pen and Ink	Give an object a pen-and-ink-like stipple or cross-hatch fill.
Stylize	Make drop shadows, add arrowheads to open lines, or round the corners of an object.
Artistic	Make a bitmapped object look like a watercolor or pastel painting, or imitate several other artistic styles.
Blur	Add Gaussian or motion blurs to an image.
Brush Strokes	Imitate different kinds of brushes.
Distort	Create distortion effects like water ripples or bathroom glass.
Noise	Apply a texture of speckling for a grainy effect.
Pixelate	Divide an image into individual dots for halftone or pointillist effects.
Sharpen	Sharpen an image.
Sketch	Imitate several drawing techniques, like charcoal, crayon, or pen and ink.
Stylize	Add glowing edges to an image.
Texture	Make an image appear cracked, grainy, patched, made of stained glass, etc.
Video	Change a video still color mode.

NOTE

Most of the Photoshop (or raster) filters and effects can be used only on imported or placed raster or bitmapped RGB images, such as photographs, and won't work on vector objects created directly in the Illustrator program.

Applying a Filter

OK, so let's do something with a filter and see what happens. You can use this little trick to create snowflakes for your next Christmas card. Create a six-point star on the artboard.

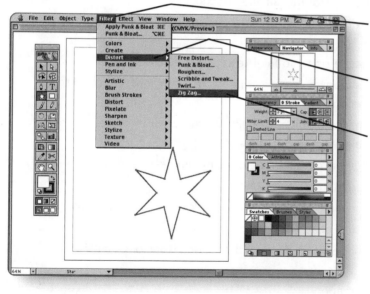

1. Click on **Filter**. The Filter menu will open.

2. Click on **Distort**. The Distort submenu will open.

3. Click on **Zig Zag**. The menus will close and the Zig Zag dialog box will appear.

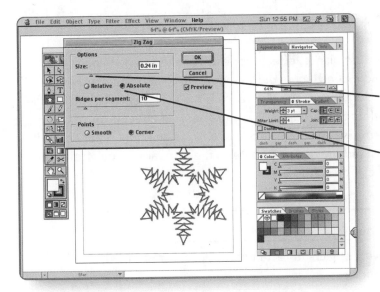

4. Click in the **Preview check box**. You will be able to preview the filter commands.

5. Drag the **Size slider**. The size of the zigzags will change.

6. Click on the **Absolute option button**. The zigzags will be confined to the original shape of the object.

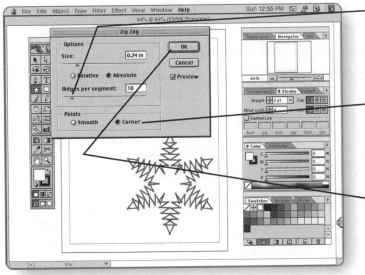

7. Drag the **Ridges per segment slider**. The number of zigzags on each line will change.

8. Click on the **Smooth or Corner Points option button**. The corner points will be rounded or angled.

9. Click on **OK**. The dialog box will close and the filter will be applied to the object.

Effects

At first glance, effects appear to do the same thing as filters—and indeed, some of them do have the same commands and dialog boxes. The difference is the way Illustrator applies the effect to the object. Illustrator sees an effect in much the same way it sees a stroke or a fill; as an effect is applied, it is also added as an attribute to the Appearance palette so that it can be edited even after it has been applied and saved.

Group	Includes Effects That
Convert to Shape	Convert objects to rectangles, ellipses, or rounded rectangles.
Distort And Transform	Offer the same commands as the Distort filters, plus the Transform dialog box.
Path	Let you offset a path or outline a stroke or object.
Pathfinder	Offer all the commands from the Pathfinder palette.
Rasterize	Turn vector objects into raster images.
Stylize	Round off corners, create drop shadows, add inner or outer glows, create feathering, and add arrowheads to lines.

Applying an Effect

When you apply an effect to an object, the effect is visible, but the underlying structure of the object doesn't change. Create another star object to work with. Keep it selected.

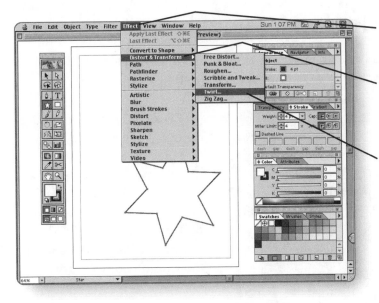

1. Click on **Effect**. The Effect menu will open.

2. Click on **Distort & Transform**. The Distort & Transform submenu will open.

3. Click on **Twirl**. The menus will close, and the Twirl dialog box will appear.

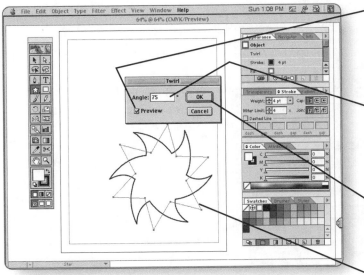

4. Click in the **Preview check box**. A check mark will appear and you will be able to preview the Effects commands.

5. Double-click in the **Angle text box** and **enter** the desired **twirl angle value**. The twirl effect will be visible.

6. Click on **OK**. The dialog box will close and the twirl effect will be applied to the star.

7. Notice that the **underlying shape** of the star is unchanged, but the twirl effect is visible.

The Inner Glow Effect

Let's add a few more effects to the selected star and work with them in the Appearance palette.

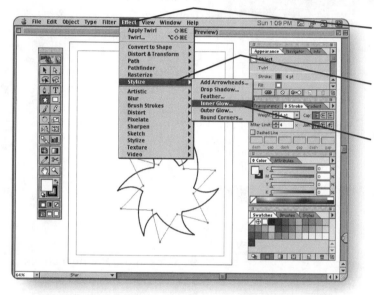

1. Click on **Effect**. The Effect menu will open.

2. Click on **Stylize**. The Stylize submenu will open.

3. Click on **Inner Glow**. The menus will close, and the Inner Glow dialog box will appear.

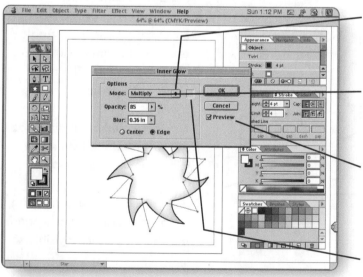

4. Click on the **Mode pop-up menu**. The pop-up menu will open.

5. Click on **Multiply**. The Multiply mode will be selected, and the menu will close.

6. Click in the **Preview check box**. A check mark will appear and the Effects commands will be visible.

7. Click on the **color box**. The Color Picker dialog box will appear.

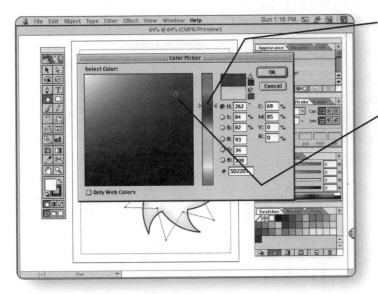

8. Click on a **color** in the multicolor strip. A range of the desired color will appear in the Select Color field.

9. Click on a **color** in the Select Color field. The color you click on will become the new color for the Inner Glow effect.

10. Click on OK. The Color Picker will close.

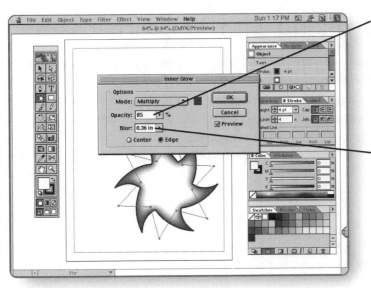

11. Double-click in the **Opacity text box**. Enter an opacity percentage value. (Or click the arrowhead button on the right of the box and adjust the slider.)

12. Double-click in the **Blur text box** and **enter** a **blur distance**. (Or click on the arrowhead button on the right of the box and adjust the slider.)

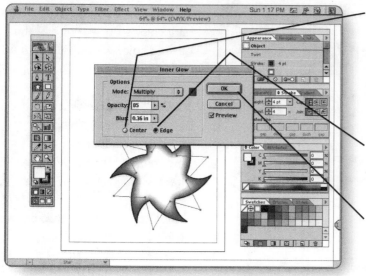

13a. Click on the **Center option button**. The glow will come from the center of the object.

OR

13b. Click on the **Edge option button**. The glow will come in from the edge of the object.

14. Click on **OK**. The dialog box will close and the effect will be applied to the object.

Working with Appearances

When you open the Appearance palette, you'll notice that all the attributes of the selected object are listed in the order they were placed. You can rearrange the stacking order of these attributes, and you can add or delete attributes and effects in the Appearance palette.

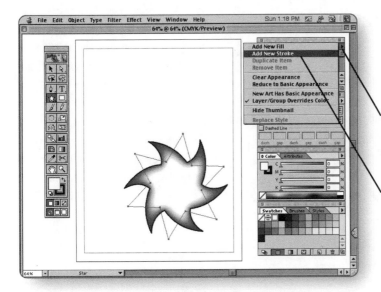

1. Click on the **Appearance tab** (if needed). The Appearance palette will move to the front.

2. Click on the **Appearance palette menu button**. The option menu will open.

3. Click on **Add New Stroke**. The menu will close and a second stroke will be added to the object with the same attributes as the first stroke. The new stroke will be listed in the Appearance palette.

Changing an Appearance Attribute

Not only can you add multiple strokes and fills to a single object, you can edit and restack them to create exactly the appearance you want.

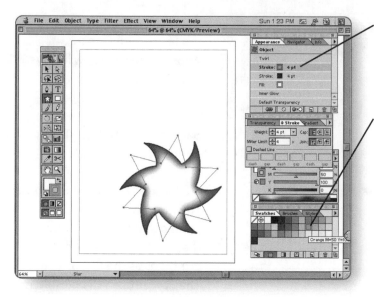

1. Click on the **new stroke title bar** in the Appearance palette. The title bar will darken and the stroke will be selected.

2. Click on a **different color swatch** in the Swatches palette. The selected stroke will change to the new color.

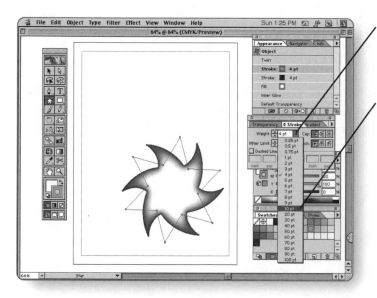

3. Click on the **Weight down arrow** in the Stroke palette. A pop-up menu will appear.

4. Click on a **new weight**. The menu will close and the new weight will be applied to the selected stroke.

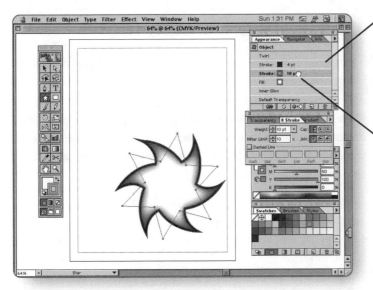

5. Click on the **stroke title bar**, and then **drag** the **mouse** downward. The cursor becomes a fist, and an outline of the title bar will move with it.

6. Move the **fist cursor** until it's between the original stroke title bar and the fill title bar; then release the mouse button. The new stroke title bar will be placed in the new location and the stroke will move backward on the object.

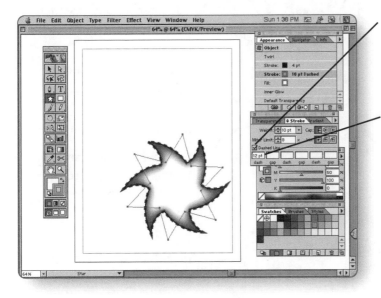

7. Click in the **Dashed Line check box** on the Stroke palette. The selected stroke will become a dashed line.

8. Enter a **point value** in the first dashed line text box. The dashed stroke will be edited appropriately.

Appearance Palette Icons

The bottom of the Appearance palette contains the following five settings icons:

- **New Art Maintains Appearance**. If this icon is not selected, any subsequent artwork is given the same appearance. If the icon is selected, it darkens and gives any new art just the default appearance.

- **Clear Appearance**. Clicking on this icon clears the appearance off of the Appearance palette, and any selected object with that appearance is given a stroke and fill of none.

- **Reduce to Basic Appearance**. Click on this icon to remove any applied appearances and reset any object to the default appearance.

- **Duplicate Selected Item**. Click on this icon to duplicate any selected attribute in the appearance.

- **Delete Selected Item**. Click on this icon to delete any selected attribute in the appearance.

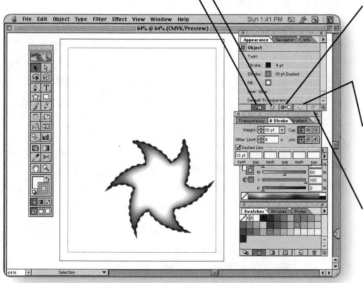

Saving an Appearance as a Style

If you create an appearance that you want to use over and over again, you can save it as a style. Styles are saved on the Styles palette, which is just like the Brush and Swatch palettes. Once you save a style, it's yours forever. Or at least until you delete it.

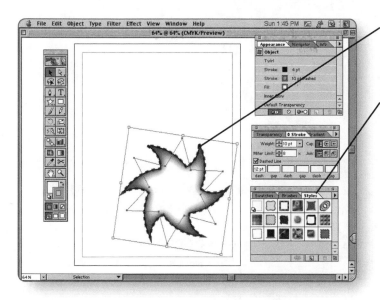

1. Click on an **object** with the new appearance. The object will be selected.

2. Click on the **Styles palette tab**. The Styles palette will move to the front.

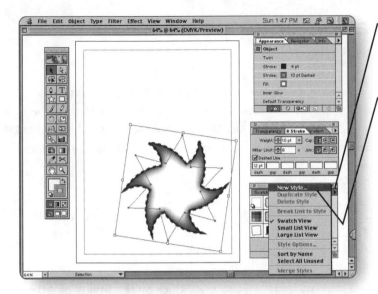

3. **Click** on the **Styles** palette menu button. The styles option menu will open.

4. **Click** on **New Style**. The menu will close and the Style Options dialog box will appear.

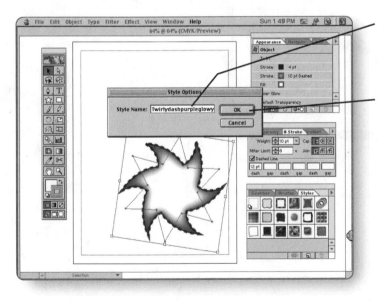

5. **Press Tab** to move to the **Style Name text box** and **type** in a **name** for the new style.

6. **Click** on **OK**. The dialog box will close and the new style icon will appear in the Styles palette.

Applying a Style to an Object

You are now ready to apply the new style to anything you want. Make sure the first icon at the bottom of the Appearance palette is selected. The button will be dark.

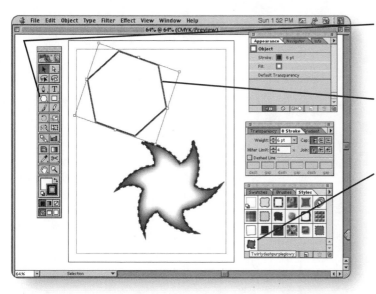

1. Click on an **object drawing tool**. The tool will become active.

2. **Click and drag** on the **artboard**. A new object will appear.

3. Click on the **new style icon** on the Styles palette. The selected object will be given the new style.

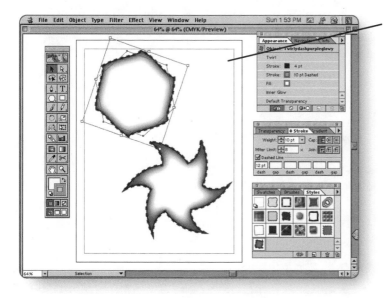

4. **Command+click** on an **empty place** on the artboard. The object will be deselected.

11

Working with Compound Paths

Back in Chapter 7, "Working with Paths and Pathfinders," you learned a lot about the Pathfinder palette. Among the tools you used from that palette were the Minus Front and Minus Back tools. If you used either of those tools to punch a hole in an object, you've already made a *compound path*—two or more paths in one object. So if you have a path describing the outside of the donut and a path describing a donut hole that you can see through, the image of the donut can be described as a compound path. In this chapter, you'll learn how to …

- Make a compound path
- Release a compound path
- Reverse the direction of a path

Creating a Compound Path

Instead of using a donut for this example, I am going to use a circular saw blade (object #1), into which I need to "cut" a notched hole (object #2) for mounting the blade onto the saw. Through the hole in the blade, you will be able to see a board (object #3). You can use whatever images you want, but you do need to do a bit of setup before you begin the exercise:

1. **Create** three different **objects** and give them different fills.

NOTE

Your objects don't have to be as fancy as the ones in this chapter—I just thought you'd like some cool stuff to look at while you work. Basic shapes that you learned to create in Chapter 3 and learned to fill in Chapter 8 will be fine.

---

2. **Stack** the **objects** one in front of another, with the smallest object in front of the other two. (The rear object isn't really necessary, but it will help you visualize the process.)

3. **Make sure** the **outer edges** of the front object are completely inside the boundary of the object directly behind it.

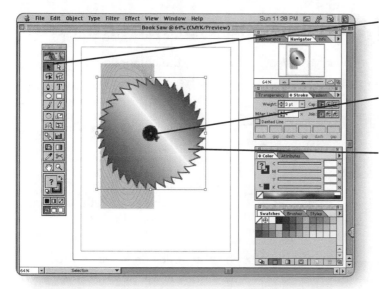

1. Click on the **Selection tool** (or the Lasso tool). The tool will become active.

2. Click on the **front object**. The object will be selected.

3. Shift-click on the **object directly behind** the front object. Both objects will be selected.

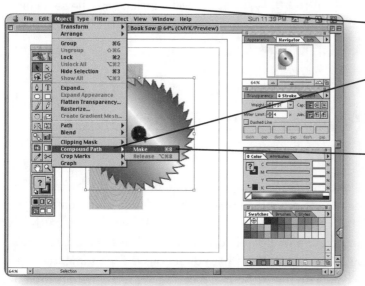

4. Click on **Object**. The Object menu will open.

5. Click on **Compound Path**. The Compound Path submenu will open.

6. Click on **Make**. The menus will close and the two objects will become a compound path, with the front object creating a hole in the second object.

Releasing the Compound Path

If you want to *release,* or remove, the compound path, follow these steps.

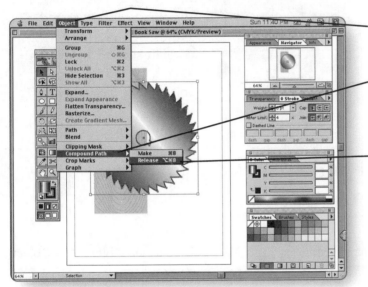

1. Click on **Object**. The Object menu will open.

2. Click on **Compound Path**. The Compound Path submenu will open.

3. Click on **Release**. The menus will close and the compound path will become two separate paths. The hole will be filled with the same fill attributes as the second object.

Reversing the Direction of a Path

All of the paths in Illustrator have a direction. In the case of a closed path around an object, the direction of the path is either clockwise or counterclockwise. When the two paths of a compound path point in opposite directions, the object on top forms a hole. If the path directions are the same, there is no hole. Use the Attributes palette to reverse the direction of an existing path. The results are similar to creating and releasing a compound path.

Before beginning the next exercise, redo the compound path so that a hole is present.

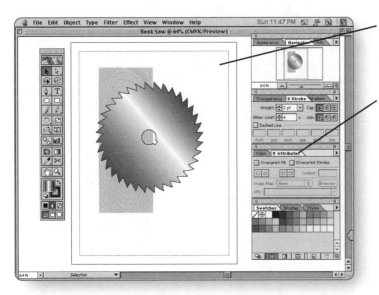

1. **Command+click** on an **empty place** on the artboard. The object will be deselected.

2. **Click** on the **Attributes palette tab**. The Attributes palette will move to the front.

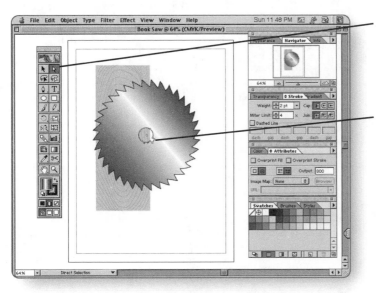

3. **Click** on the **Direct Selection tool**. The Direct Selection tool will become active.

4. **Click** on the **hole object path** in the compound path. It will be selected.

5. **Click** on the **Reverse Path Direction Off** button on the Attributes palette. The path will be refilled.

6. **Click** on the **Reverse Path Direction On** button in the Attributes palette. The hole will be restored.

12

Working with Masks

An airbrush artist uses something called a *frisket* to shield his painting from overspray and to paint shapes and hard edges with the airbrush. A frisket is like a very low-adhesive contact paper made in clear plastic sheets or rolls. The artist lays the frisket over his drawing, then cuts holes in it with a knife to expose the areas he wants to paint. This technique is the principle behind *masking* in Illustrator—except on the computer, you lay down the color first and then eliminate whatever is sticking outside the boundaries of the desired shape of the mask. Cool, huh? It beats using actual masking tape, that's for sure! In this chapter, you will learn how to…

- Make a clipping mask
- Release a clipping mask
- Make an opacity mask
- Edit an opacity mask

Making a Clipping Mask

In Illustrator 9, the basic mask command is called a *clipping mask*, because it's used to clip away the extraneous material behind it. Follow these steps to see how the clipping mask works.

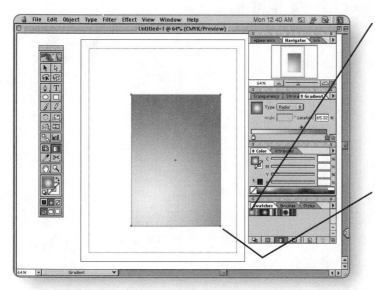

1. Create a **new gradient** or click on a **gradient swatch** on the Swatches palette. The swatch will be selected.

2. Click on the **Rectangle tool.** The rectangle tool will be selected.

3. Click and drag diagonally on the artboard. A rectangle will appear with the desired fill.

NOTE

Understand that this gradient is just an example. You can use any background to fill a clipping mask. You can create blends or textures. Use several different-colored objects, a pattern, columns of type, or even raster images and photographs to fill a mask.

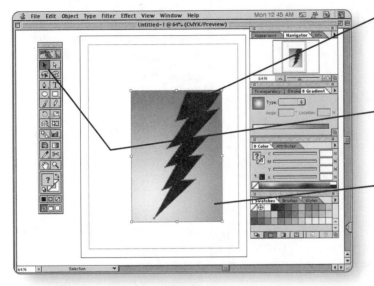

4. **Create** or **paste** a **second object** on the artboard. Position the new object in front of the filled object.

5. **Click** on the **Selection** or **Lasso tool**. The tool will be active.

6. **Shift-click**, **marquee**, or **lasso** both the **rectangle** and the **new object**. Both objects will be selected.

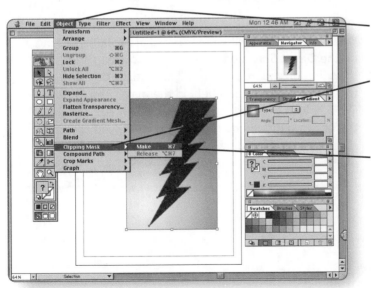

7. **Click** on **Object**. The Object menu will open.

8. **Click** on **Clipping Mask**. The Clipping Mask submenu will open.

9. **Click** on **Make**. The menus will close and the attributes of the rear object will only be visible only within the boundaries of the masking object.

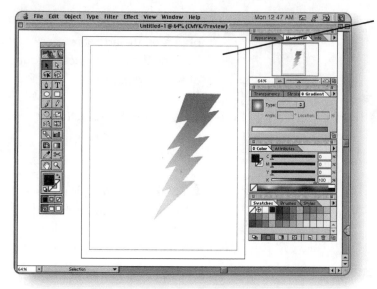

10. **Command+click** on an **empty place** on the artboard. The masked object will be deselected.

TIP

You can edit and tweak the masked artwork by clicking on the Direct Selection tool and then clicking and dragging on the mask. You will essentially be moving the background around behind the mask. The mask is like a hole in the artboard through which you can view the background. If you release the mask, you can add or subtract anything you want, and then remake the mask over and over again. HooAhhh!!

Releasing the Mask

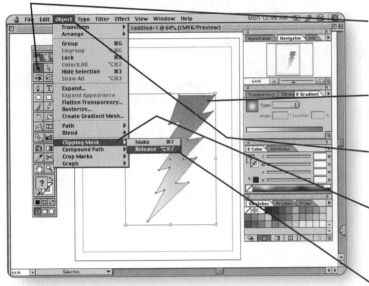

1. Click on the **Selection tool**. The Selection tool will be active.

2. Click on the **masked object**. It will be selected.

3. Click on **Object**. The Object menu will open.

4. Click on **Clipping Mask**. The Clipping Mask submenu will open.

5. Click on **Release**. The menus will close and the masked object will become two separate objects again.

Making an Opacity Mask

An opacity mask (or *transparency* mask, if your glass is half empty) is very slick. You can make an opacity mask with a gradient, then use it to fade an object into the background. The opacity mask uses the color of an object as a transparency map. The lighter the color, the more transparent it becomes. It's really easier to see than describe, so let's do one. Before you start, click on the Stroke box and click on None; then click on the Fill box to bring it to the front.

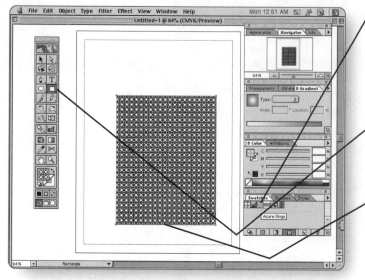

1. **Click** on the **Azure Rings** default pattern swatch in the Swatches palette. The swatch will be selected as a fill attribute.

2. **Click** on the **Rectangle tool**. The Rectangle tool will become active.

3. **Click and drag** a **rectangle** on the artboard. The rectangle will have the Azure Ring fill. Do not deselect it.

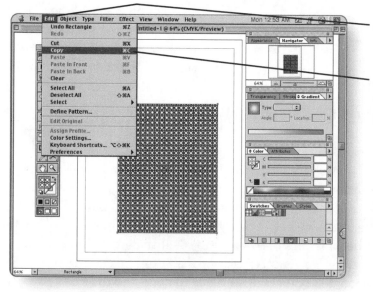

4. **Click** on **Edit**. The Edit menu will open.

5. **Click** on **Copy**. The menu will close and the rectangle will be copied to the Clipboard.

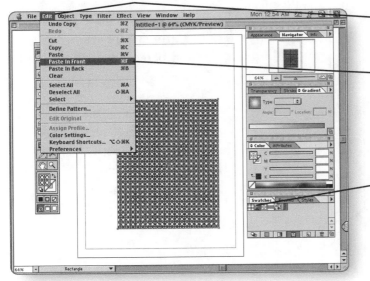

6. Click on **Edit**. The Edit menu will open.

7. Click on **Paste In Front**. The menu will close and a selected copy of the rectangle will be pasted directly in front of the original.

8. Click on the **White, Black linear gradient** on the Swatches palette. The top rectangle will be filled with the gradient fill.

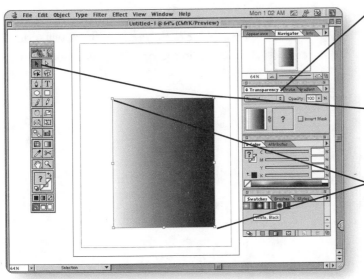

9. Click on the **Transparency palette tab** (if necessary). The Transparency palette will move to the front.

10. Click on the **Selection tool**. The Selection tool will be active.

11. Click and drag the pointer across the rectangle and release the mouse button. Both rectangles will be selected.

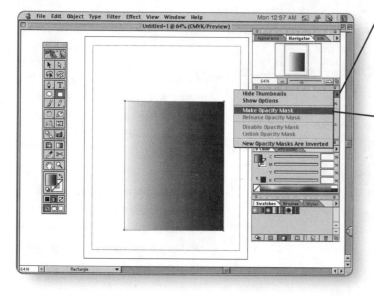

12. Click on the **Transparency palette menu button**. The Transparency palette menu will open.

13. Click on **Make Opacity Mask**. The two rectangles will become an opacity mask, with the Azure Ring pattern fading into the background.

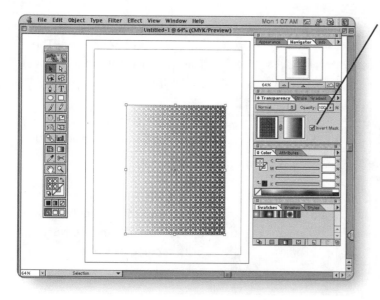

14. Click in the **Invert Mask check box**. The mask will fade in the opposite direction.

Editing an Opacity Mask

The bad news is you can't just click and drag the opacity mask with the Direct Selection tool to edit it like you can with a regular mask. The good news is you can edit the opacity mask from the Transparency palette. Make sure the object is still selected.

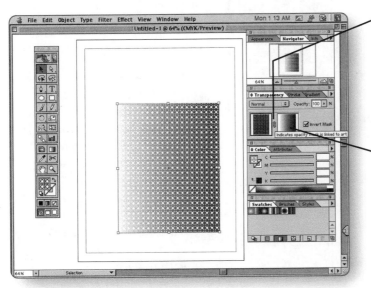

1. **Click** on the **Link icon** between the thumbnails of the artwork and the mask. The icon will disappear and the artwork and the gradient will no longer be linked.

2. **Click** on the **gradient thumbnail.** It will be outlined in black and ready to edit.

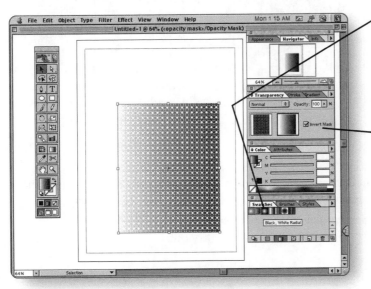

3. **Click** on the **Black, White Radial gradient.** The thumbnail gradient will change to a radial gradient, and the artwork will have a radial fade.

4. **Click** in the **Invert Mask check box** to uncheck it (if desired). The gradient will be inverted.

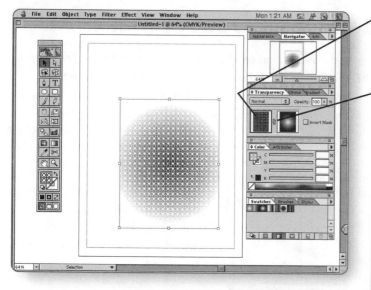

5. **Click** on the **artwork thumbnail**. It will be selected and outlined in black.

6. **Click** in the **space** between the thumbnails. The link icon will reappear and the opacity mask will be linked again.

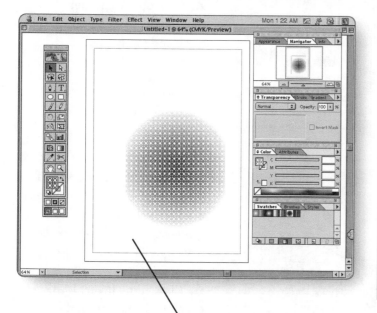

7. **Command+click** on an **empty place** on the artboard. The object will be deselected, and the thumbnails will disappear from the Transparency palette.

13

Digging through the Layers

You already know that you can move objects backward and forward to place them in front of or behind one another. With the Layers palette, you can take this capability even further. You'd be surprised at how many individual pieces can accumulate in even the simplest image. Working in multiple layers greatly simplifies a complex project by allowing you to lock out or even hide any of the other elements of your picture while you work on or develop another one. You can make your artwork as complex as you want and divide it into as many layers and sublayers as your computer's memory will allow. In this chapter, you will learn how to …

- Create new layers and choose their options
- Arrange and restack layers
- Lock, hide, and select layers
- Create sublayers
- Merge, flatten, and delete layers

Creating a New Layer

Before you made your first mark on the Illustrator artboard, you had already created your first layer. You can't have a document without having a default layer to start with. After that, you can create layers and then put the artwork on them, or create the artwork first. You can divide the layers into color fills, similar strokes, backgrounds, styles, types, or whatever makes organizing the image most comfortable to you. So let's open the Layers palette, create a few layers, and start organizing this mess. To begin, create or place an object like this club symbol and deselect it.

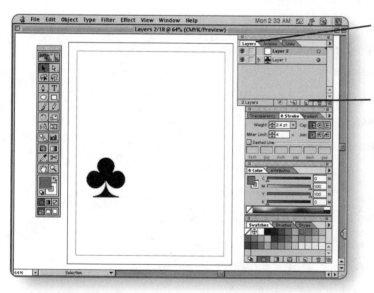

1. Click on the **Layers palette tab** (if needed). The Layers palette will move to the front.

2. Click on the **Create New Layer icon** at the bottom of the Layers palette. A new layer will be created, and its title bar will be highlighted in the Layers palette.

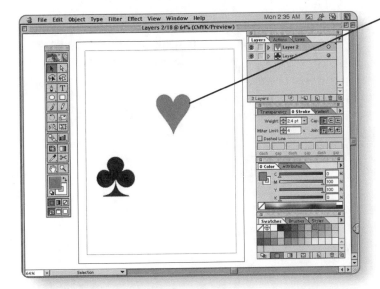

3. **Draw** or **place** another **object** on the artboard. A thumbnail of the object will appear on the selected layer's title bar. Repeat steps 2 and 3 until you have four objects in four different layers.

Controlling Layer Options

The Layer Options dialog box will let you name each layer and apply any other options you might deem necessary.

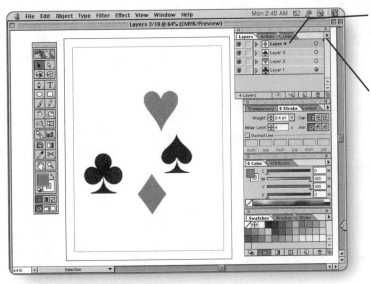

1. **Click** on a **layer title bar** in the Layers palette. The layer will be selected.

2. **Click** on the **Layers palette menu button**. The Layers palette menu will appear.

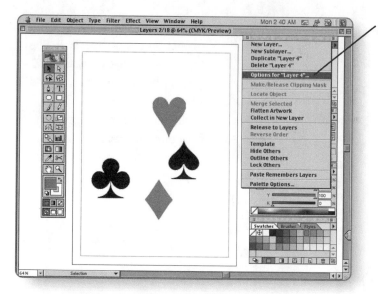

3. **Click** on **Options for**. The menu will close, and the Layer Options dialog box will appear.

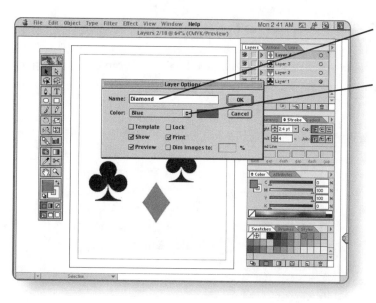

4. **Enter** a **name** for the layer in the Name text box.

5. **Click** on the **Color pop-up menu** (if needed). The menu will open.

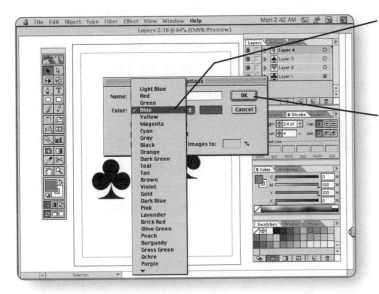

6. Click on a **color**. A check mark will appear to the left of that color, which will be selected for the layer.

7. Click on **OK**. The dialog box will close and the layer name will appear on the layer title bar next to the thumbnail.

NOTE

The color selected in the Layers Option dialog box will be the color of the path lines, anchor points, handles, and bounding boxes for all the objects in that layer.

This exercise only scratches the surface of layers and how you can use them to your advantage. For a detailed study on layers, consult the Adobe Help system.

Restacking the Layers

After an image or groups of images have been assigned to their respective layers, you can shuffle the layers any way you want. Move the objects so that they overlap each other and deselect them.

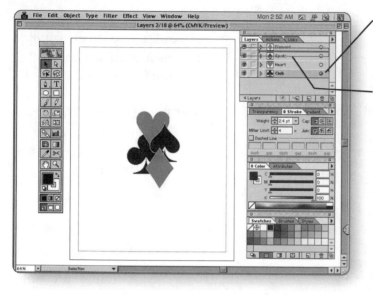

1. **Click and hold** on the **title bar** of the bottommost layer. The layer will be selected.

2. **Drag upward.** The cursor will become a fist holding a ghosted image of the title bar.

3. **Continue dragging** the **fist cursor** until it is between two other layer title bars, and **release** the **mouse button.** The layer will move to the new position in the Layers palette, and the object represented by the title bar will be restacked accordingly on the artboard.

Hiding and Showing the Layers

When layers overlap each other and you want to be able to see the objects on the hidden layer, you can make other layers invisible by clicking on the toggle visibility box.

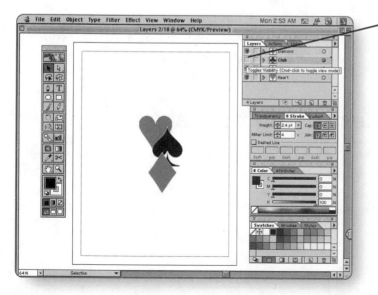

1. **Click** on the **Visibility option box** (the box with the eye icon). The eye in the box and the image represented by the layer title will disappear.

2. **Click** on the **Visibility option box** again. The image and the icon will reappear.

Locking a Layer

It's a good idea to lock a layer so that the objects on it cannot be accidentally edited.

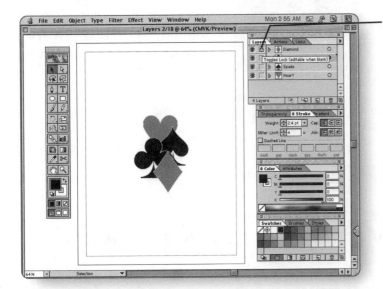

1. Click on the **option box** on the right of the Visibility box in the Layers palette.

A padlock icon will appear in the box, and the layer represented by that title bar will be uneditable.

2. Click on the **option box** again. The padlock icon will disappear and the corresponding layer will be unlocked and editable.

Selecting a Layer

After you develop an illustration with several layers, you might want to select only the objects on a particular layer. You'll need to do this to edit or manipulate any objects on that layer, which you'll learn about in the next few sections.

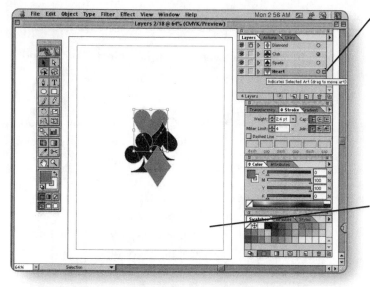

1. **Click** to the **right** of the small circle on the title bar of the layer you want to select. A small square will appear in the title bar in the color that was assigned to that layer. All the objects on that layer will be selected in a common bounding box.

2. **Command+click anywhere.** The layer will be deselected, and the small box in the title bar will disappear.

Moving Art between Layers

You may need to move one or more pieces of art from one layer to another. This is also done in the Layers palette.

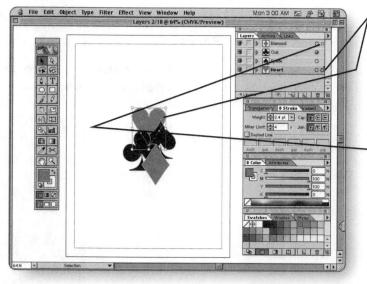

1. **Click and hold** on the **Select Art button** on the far right side of the title bar. A selection box will appear and the layer object(s) will be selected.

2. **Drag** the **selection box** vertically into another title bar and **release** the **mouse button**. The contents of the layer move to the new layer, and the object(s) appears in the thumbnail on that layer. The selection box acquires the color assigned to the new layer.

Working with Sublayers

In the preceding exercise, we created a sublayer (surprise!). A *sublayer* is a layer within a layer, so in that example, the heart shape became a sublayer of the diamond shape top layer. You can do anything with a sublayer that you can do with the whole layer. You can restack sublayers within the layer, for example, or drag a sublayer out of one layer into another. You can lock, hide, or edit sublayers and create as many as your computer will allow. The beauty of using sublayers is that you can manage your entire image from within the Layers palette.

Moving a Sublayer into Another Layer

Now we'll put our heart back where it belongs.

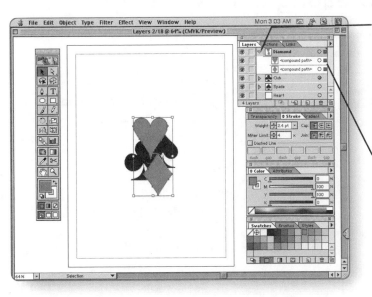

1. **Click** on the **arrowhead pointer** on the left side of the thumbnail in the title bar. The arrowhead will point downward, and the sublayer title bars will open.

2. **Click** on the **Select Art button** in the sublayer you want to move.

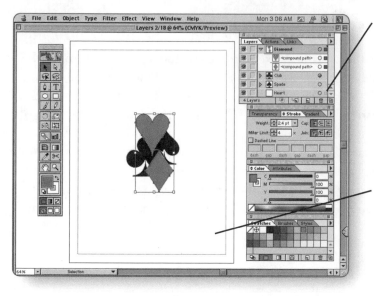

3. Drag the **selection box** to the title bar of the layer you want to use and **release** the **mouse button**. The contents of the sublayer will be moved to the original layer, and the selection box will return to the color assigned to that layer.

4. **Command+click anywhere** on the artboard. The sublayers will be deselected.

Creating a New Sublayer

You can create an empty sublayer the same way you created an empty layer.

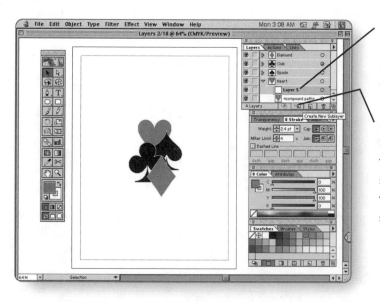

1. Click on the **title bar** of the layer under which you want to put the new sublayer. The layer will be selected.

2. **Click** on the **Create New Sublayer icon** at the bottom of the Layers palette. The new sublayer will appear below the title bar of the layer you selected.

Deleting a Layer or Sublayer

You may sometimes find yourself overwhelmed by all the layers and sublayers and want to simplify things a bit. Or you may have empty layers and sublayers to get rid of after you move, merge, and manage a few of them.

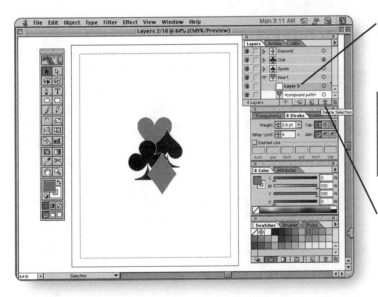

1. Click on the **title bar** of the layer you want to delete. The layer will be selected.

2. Click on the **Delete Selection icon** in the lower right corner of the Layers palette. The layer will be deleted.

Merging Layers

Merging layers together will put all the selected layers and sublayers into one layer and eliminates the empty layers from the Layers palette.

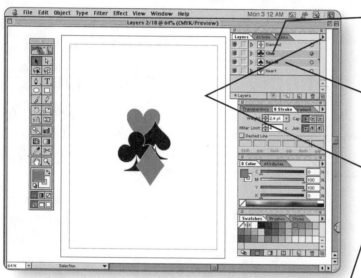

1. **Click** on a **title bar** in the Layers palette. The layer will be selected.

2. **Shift-click** on a **second title bar**. That layer will also be selected.

3. **Click** on the **Layers palette menu button**. The menu will open.

4. **Click** on **Merge Selected**. The menu will close and the selected layers and their sublayers will merge into the uppermost selected layer. The artwork in all selected layers and sublayers will be visible in that uppermost layer's thumbnail. All empty layers will be deleted.

NOTE

You can merge as many layers and sublayers as you want. Command-click on nonadjacent layers to select them before merging.

Undoing the Merge

If you change your mind, there's only one way to undo a merge. Fortunately, it only takes a second.

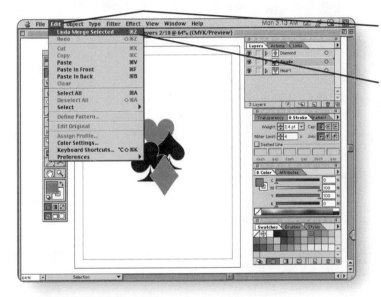

1. Click on **Edit**. The Edit menu will open.

2. Click on **Undo Merge Selected**. The menu will close and the merged layers will return to their former places in the Layers palette.

Flattening the Artwork

After you finish your masterpiece, you might want to flatten it. *Flattening* the artwork puts all the layers and sublayers into a single layer.

CAUTION

After you flatten the artwork and then save and close the drawing, you cannot undo; be sure that's what you really want to do.

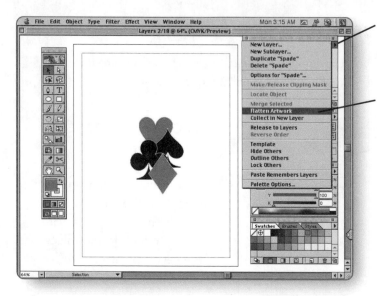

1. Click on the **Layers palette menu button**. The menu will open.

2. Click on **Flatten Artwork**. The menu will close and all the layers and sublayers will be moved to a single layer.

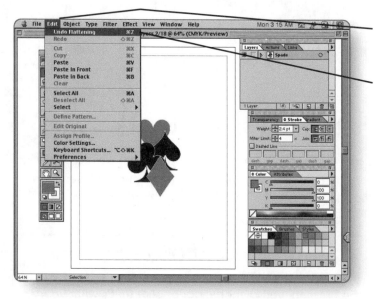

3. Click on **Edit**. The Edit menu will open.

4. Click on **Undo Flattening**. The menu will close and the layers will return to their former places in the Layers palette.

14

Getting a Word In

Adobe Illustrator has a secret identity! In the previous 13 chapters, you discovered what a terrific drawing and illustration tool this application is. But Illustrator also has a set of text tools that you would only find on a full-blown word processor or page layout program. Add to that the fact that, with Illustrator, you also have the ability to turn the words into objects, and hey, you already know what you can do with objects, for crying out loud! I mean, if a picture is worth a thousand words, a picture with words must be worth ten times that, right? Feel free to be a little giddy at this point.

This chapter is all about text and type, so this is where you'll learn about …

- The Type tools
- The Character palette
- The Paragraph palette
- Converting text to paths

Putting the Text on the Page with the Type Tools

There are six Type tools that you can use to put words, letters, and numbers on the page. The primary three follow:

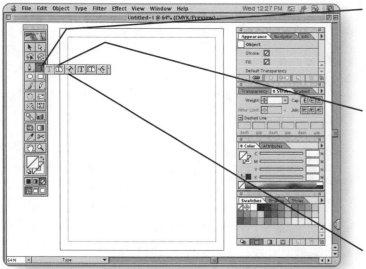

- The **Type tool** creates a point from which you can begin a line of type. This is the most often-used Type insertion tool.

- The **Area Type tool** is the tool you use to fill the confines of an object with text. When the text hits the inside edge of the object, it automatically "wraps" or starts a new line.

- The **Path Type tool** places type along any path.

The other three Type tools are the same as the first three, except they place type vertically instead of horizontally:

- The **Vertical Type tool** stacks letters on top of each other.

- The **Vertical Area Type tool** stacks letters on top of each other inside an object area.

- The **Vertical Path Type tool** places letters vertically along a path. Oh, the possibilities!

First let's open the Character pallet, and then we'll put some type on the page.

Opening the Character Palette

We won't get into the palettes right away, but let's get them out on the work area, because all the Type tools, palettes, and menus really work in combination with each other.

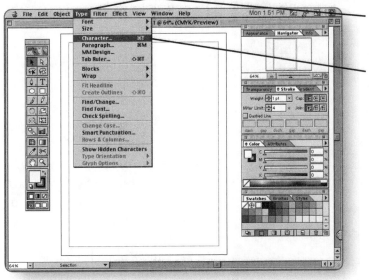

1. Click on **Type**. The Type menu will open.

2. Click on **Character**. The menu will close and the Character palette will appear on the work area.

Introducing the Type Tool

The Type tool lets you start typing at one point, and if you don't press Return, your line of type will go right through the side of your monitor. Okay, okay, that's not quite true—but you will have to hit the Return key to start a second line.

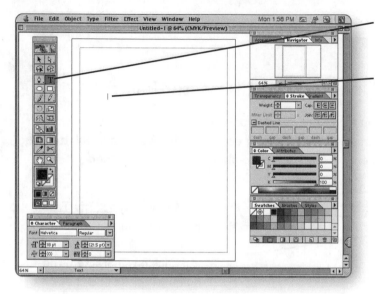

1. Click on the **Type tool**. The tool will become active.

2. Click in the **area** on the artboard where you want the text to begin. The Type tool cursor will disappear and a text marker will start blinking.

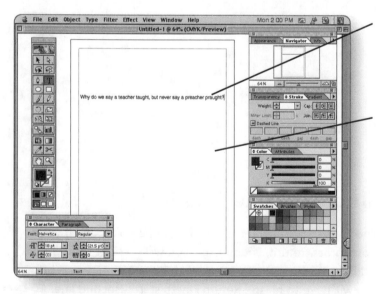

3. Begin typing. The type will begin at the point you selected. (You must hit the Return key to start a second line.)

4. Command+click on an **empty place** on the artboard. The object will be deselected.

Setting Type in a Rectangle

You can use the Type tool to create a rectangular type block. These blocks are very handy for making columns, which I'll talk about later in the chapter.

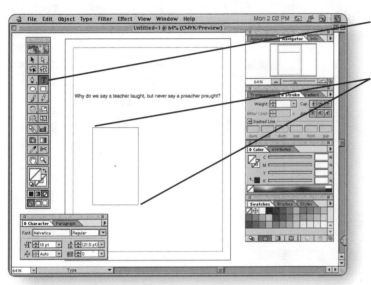

1. Click on the **Type tool**. The Type tool will become active.

2. **Click and drag** diagonally on the **artboard** while holding down the mouse button. A rectangle will appear.

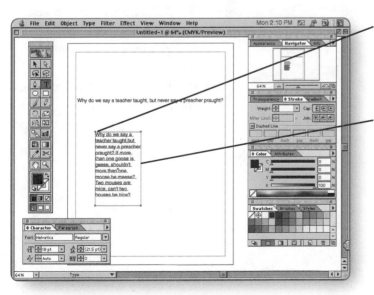

3. **Release** the **mouse button**. A blinking text insertion marker will appear in the upper left corner of the rectangle.

4. **Begin typing**. The type will stay within the confines of the rectangle, and new lines of type will automatically begin.

Creating Area Type

When you want to put a block of type inside a shape other than a rectangle, you need to use the Area Type tool.

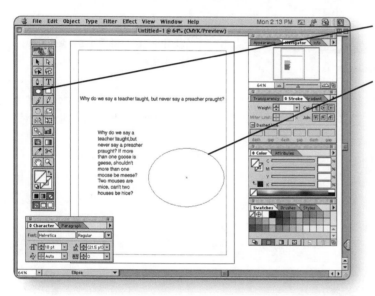

1. **Click** on the **Ellipse tool**. The tool will become active.

2. **Click and drag** anywhere on the **artboard** and **release** the **mouse button**. An elliptical shape will appear.

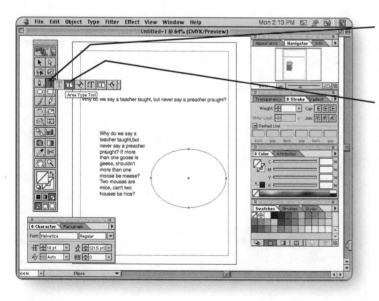

3. **Click and hold** the **mouse button** on the Type tool. A pop-up menu will open.

4. **Point** to the **Area Type tool** and **release** the **mouse button**. The pop-up will menu close and the tool will become active.

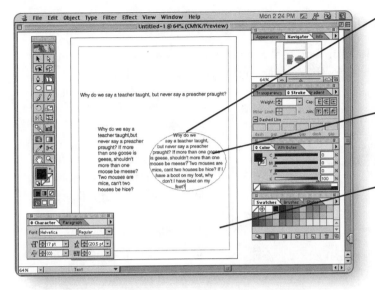

5. **Click** on the **ellipse path**. The blinking text insertion marker will appear near the top of the ellipse.

6. **Begin typing.** The text will fill the internal area of the ellipse.

7. **Command+click** on an **empty place** on the artboard. The object will be deselected.

TIP

Of course, the Area Type tool will work with any object shape, but it is more effective with more regular shapes. Trying to fill a star with many points and acute angles won't work as well as using a shape that's more open. Using a smaller type size will fill the shape with more detail than a larger type size. Experiment and play!

Setting Type on a Path

The Path Type tool enables you to type along any open or closed path. You can make type run around a border, a spiral, or any other path you create. Draw a circle with the Ellipse tool and leave it selected.

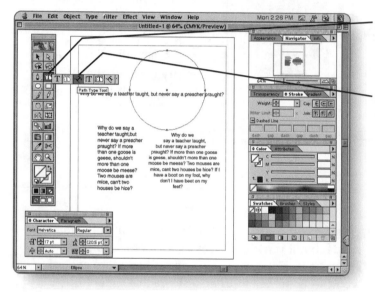

1. Click and hold the mouse button on the Type tool. A pop-up palette will appear.

2. Point to the Path Type tool and release the mouse button. The pop-up palette will close and the tool will become active.

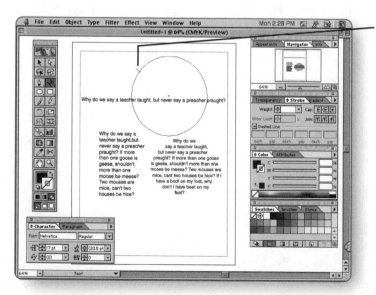

3. Point and click anywhere on the path of the circle. A blinking text insertion marker will appear.

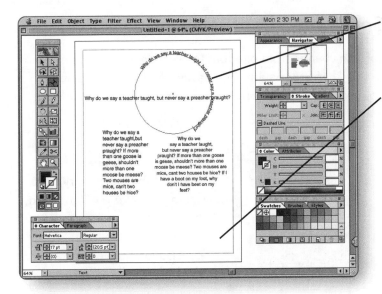

4. **Begin typing.** The line of type will follow the path of the circle as you type.

5. **Command+click** on an **empty place** on the artboard. The object will be deselected.

TIP

You can move type on a path by clicking on it with the Selection or Direct Selection tool and dragging on the I-beam that precedes the first letter in the line. The line of type will follow along the path like a train on a track. If you want to flip the type to the other side of the path, you can drag the I-beam across the path or just double-click the path.

Working with the Character Palette

On the Character palette, you will select the different type objects and control all of their measurements and spacing. To begin this exercise, select the Type tool, create a small rectangle (as demonstrated previously), and enter a few lines of type. Keep the rectangle selected.

Selecting a Font

You can change from one font to another with the Type menu or the Character palette, but having the Character palette open keeps all the information readily displayed in the work area.

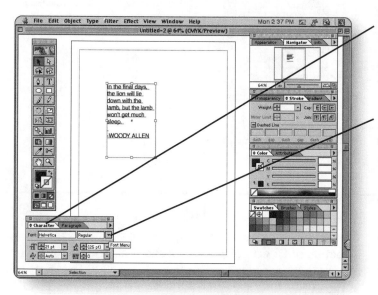

1. **Click** on the **Character palette tab** (if necessary). The Character palette will move to the front.

2. **Click** on the **Font down arrow**. The Font menu will open.

NOTE

Because no two font menus are alike, yours may look nothing like this. If you have an application such as Adobe Type Reunion installed, your fonts may even appear on the menu in their individual styles.

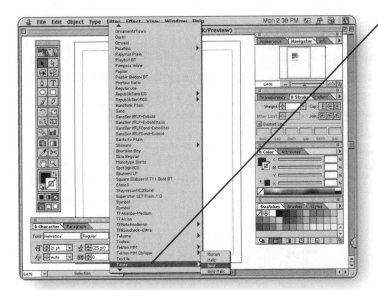

3. **Click** on the **font** you want. The font will be selected.

TIP

If the font isn't visible on the menu, move the pointer to the top or bottom of the menu, and it will scroll in that direction automatically.

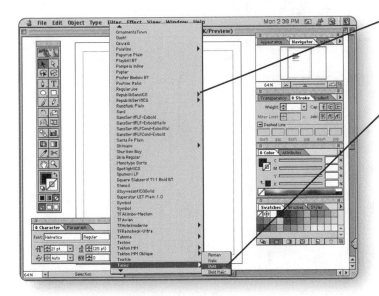

If an arrowhead is displayed to the right of the font name, a Font Style submenu will appear when the font is highlighted.

4. **Click** on the **desired font style**. The menus will close, and the font and style will be applied to any selected font on the artboard.

Changing the Font Size

The size of a typeface is determined from top to bottom with tiny units of measurement called *points*. There are 72 points to an inch, and the most common sizes for text are supplied in a drop-down menu in the Character palette.

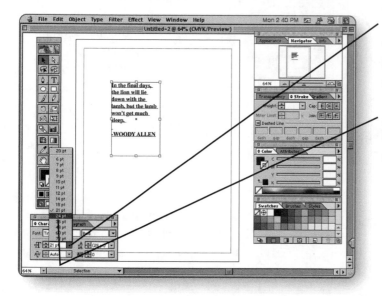

1. **Click** on the **down arrow** to the right of the Font Size text box. The default size menu will open.

2. **Click** on the **point size** you want. The new size will be applied to the selected type.

Working with Leading

Leading (rhymes with *heading*) is the measurement between two lines of type. Illustrator automatically selects a default leading for the size and style of the type, but you can change it to squeeze the lines closer together or to spread them apart.

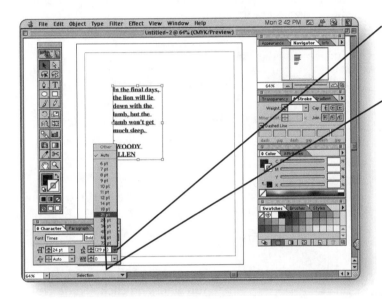

1. Click on the **Leading down arrow**. The Leading menu will open.

2. Click on the **new leading size**. The menu will close and the new leading size will be applied to the selected type.

NOTE

As with every other command on the Character palette (and many others), you have the choice of using the drop-down menu, entering a new number value in the text box, or clicking the up and down arrow buttons on the left of the text box for incremental point increases or decreases.

One Good Kern Deserves Another

Kerning is the adjustment of the space between two adjacent letters and is best practiced on larger size type. If you are designing a logo or letterhead that contains a single word or name, for instance, you might want to adjust the kerning between a few of the letters to improve the overall shape of the word. In this example, we'll tighten the kerning between the *W* and the *O* in *WOODY*.

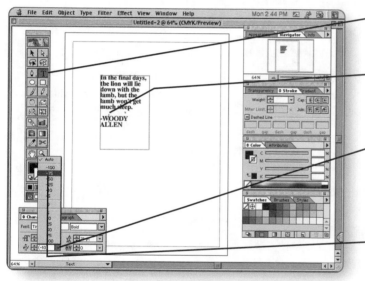

1. Click on the **Type tool**. It will become active.

2. Click between the **letters** you want to kern. The blinking insertion marker will appear.

3. Click on the **Kerning down arrow** in the Character palette. The Kerning menu will appear.

4. Point to the **kerning value** you want and **click**. (Negative numbers move the letters closer together; positive numbers move them apart.) The menu will close and the kerning will be applied to the space.

TIP

My favorite way to kern is to start with the first two steps in this example, and then hold down the Option key while hitting the left-arrow key to kern tighter or the right-arrow key to open the kerning wider. This method allows you to see the effect of the kerning on-the-fly.

Baseline Shifting

The *baseline* is that long white chalk line between first base and home plate, right? Well, yeah—among other things. But this book isn't about baseball. So for us, a baseline is the line that a letter sits on. Typically, if the type is on a path, the path is on the baseline. There are times when you'll want to move the type up or down on the baseline. To do this from the Character palette, you'll have to show the palette options. Be sure you have your text object selected before you begin this exercise.

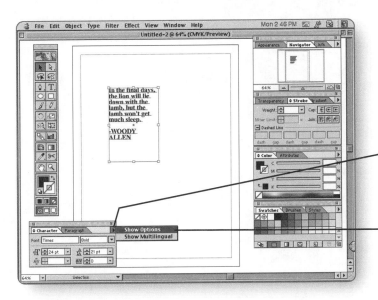

1. **Click** on the **Character palette menu button**. The options submenu will open.

2. **Click** on **Show Options**. The menu will close and the palette options will appear below the palette.

3. **Click** on the **down arrow** to the right of the Baseline shift text box. The menu will open.

4. **Click** on the **baseline shift value** you want. The selected baselines will move accordingly. Leave the object selected to continue to the next exercise.

Controlling Tracking

Tracking is pretty much the same as kerning, but instead of adjusting a single space, you're adjusting a string of spaces between several letters.

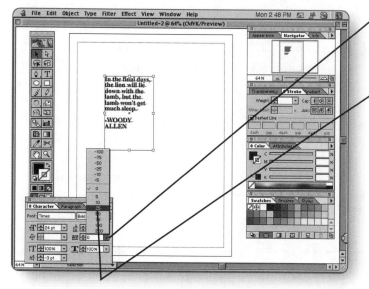

1. Click on the **Tracking down arrow**. The Tracking menu will open.

2. Click on the **tracking value** you want. The menu will close and the tracking will be applied to the text.

Vertical and Horizontal Scaling

You've scaled objects, so why not letters? That's pretty much what scaling is—stretching or squashing type. You probably shouldn't get too carried away with this one, however, or your type could become unreadable in a hurry. Select the text object before you try this technique.

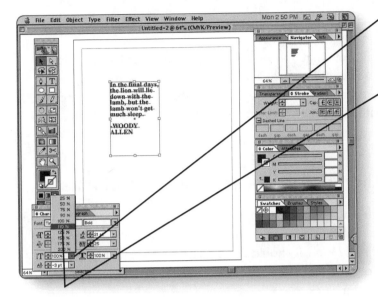

1. **Click** on the **Vertical Scaling down arrow**. The menu will open.

2. **Click** on a **number value** other than 100%. The menu will close and the vertical scaling will be applied.

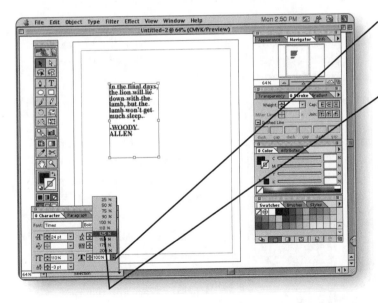

3. **Click** on the **Horizontal Scaling down arrow**. The menu will open.

4. **Click** on a **number value** other than 100%. The menu will close and the horizontal scaling will be applied.

Using the Paragraph Palette

Well, now that you've got all those individual letters and words under control, let's take a look at manipulating whole paragraphs. In the Paragraph palette, you'll find the tools to justify blocks of text and adjust the spacing around the individual paragraphs.

Aligning and Justifying Text Blocks

Remember back in Chapter 6, "Working with Precision," when you used the Align palette to center, distribute, and line up objects? Well, it should come as no surprise that Illustrator also gives you that capability with whole paragraphs. Type and select a block of text.

TIP

To change only one paragraph rather than the entire text block, activate the Text tool and click anywhere in the desired paragraph before you begin step 1.

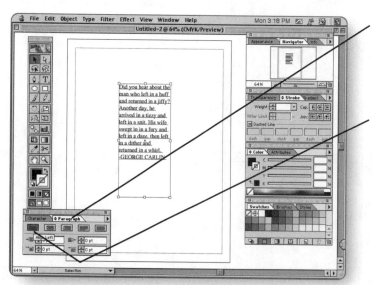

1. Click on the **Paragraph palette tab** (if necessary). The Paragraph palette will come to the front.

2. Click on **Align Left**. The selected text will align in rows flush to the left. The right side of the paragraph will be uneven.

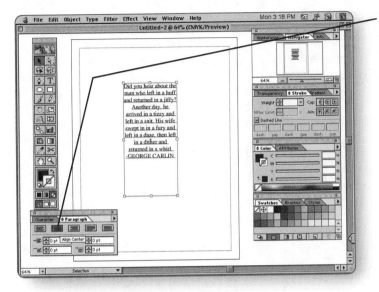

3. Click on **Align Center**. The selected text will align in the center of the rectangle, and both sides of the text block will be uneven.

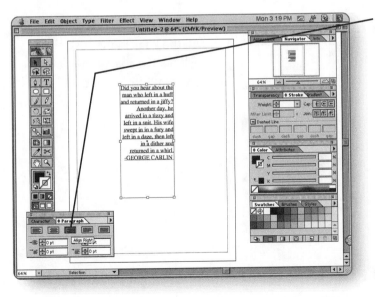

4. Click on **Align Right**. The selected text will align in rows flush to the right. The left side of the paragraph will be uneven.

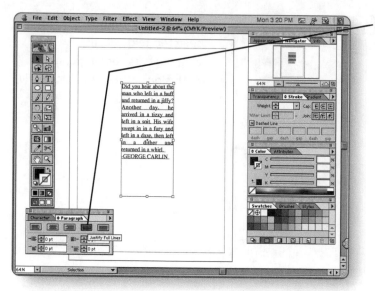

5. Click on **Justify Full Lines**. All but the last line in the text block will be word spaced to make the column flush on both sides.

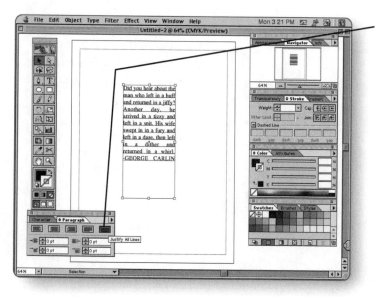

6. Click on **Justify All Lines**. All the lines in the text block will be line spaced to make the column flush on both sides.

Indenting a Text Block

Illustrator gives you the tools to indent and create space between your paragraphs. Using the same text block from the preceding exercise, use the following steps to control those parameters.

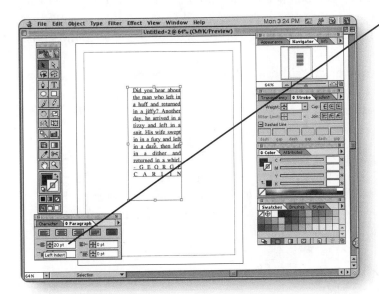

1. **Enter** a **value** in the Left Indent text box. The text block will indent to the left accordingly.

TIP

All the indent and space tools offer you the option to increase or decrease the number values in one-point increments by clicking the up or down arrow buttons on the spin buttons of the respective text windows.

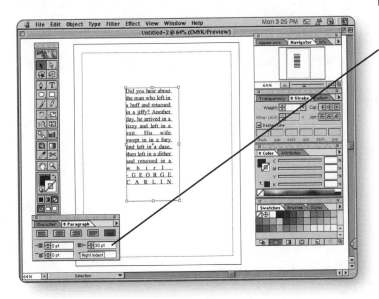

2. **Enter** a **value** in the Right Indent text box. The text block will indent to the right accordingly.

First-Line Indenting and Outdenting

Sometimes you'll want only the first line of a text block to be indented, or sometimes you'll want all but the first line to be indented (also known as a *hanging indent*). You might need to use a hanging indent to create a bulleted list or numbered list, in which the first line of the paragraph begins flush left and all remaining lines are indented. In addition to space on either side, you'll often want to add space between two paragraphs.

To demonstrate these options, type a block of text consisting of two to three paragraphs, select the text block, and follow these steps.

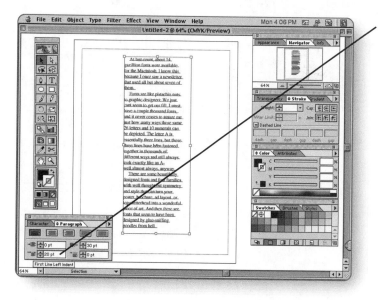

1. **Enter** a **value** (in points) in the First Line Left Indent text box. The first line of each paragraph will indent accordingly.

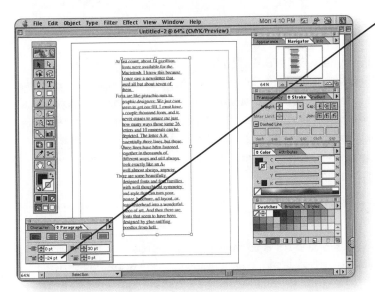

2. Enter a **negative value** (such as **-24pt**) in the First Line Left Indent text box to create a paragraph with a hanging indent.

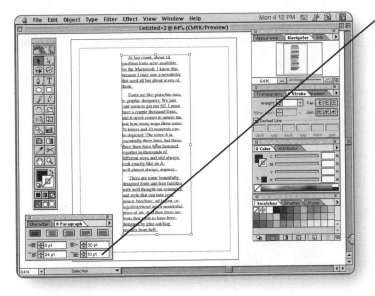

3. Enter a **value** in the Space Before Paragraph text box. The spaces between the paragraphs will adjust accordingly.

Linking the Text Blocks

Sometimes you're going to have too much type for one text block to handle, or you'll want to lay out a design that has text flowing from one block into another. Using the text block from the preceding exercise, type or paste another three to four paragraphs of text, like the gibberish shown in the illustrations. Keep typing until about half of the text overflows the box and disappears.

TIP

When text begins to overflow the borders of the existing box it's in, a small plus sign (+) appears at the end of the last visible line. This symbol indicates that there is more text than the box is allowing you to see.

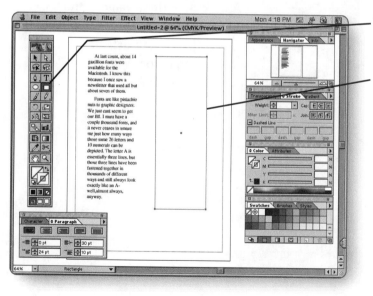

1. **Click** on the **Rectangle tool**. The tool will become active.

2. **Click and drag diagonally** on the artboard. A new rectangle will be created. (If needed, give it fill and stroke values of None.)

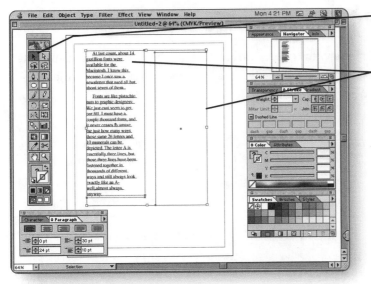

3. Click on the **Selection Tool**. The tool will become active.

4. Click and drag across (or Shift-click) both the text block and the rectangle. The objects will be selected.

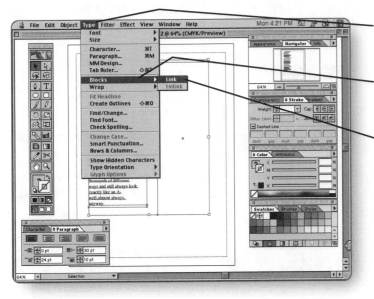

5. Click on **Type**. The Type menu will open.

6. Point to **Blocks**. The Blocks submenu will open.

7. Click on **Link**. The menus will close and the hidden text will flow into the new text block.

Resizing the Text Blocks

If the new text block doesn't get the job done, you can create as many new blocks as you need, or you can stretch the blocks to fit the type.

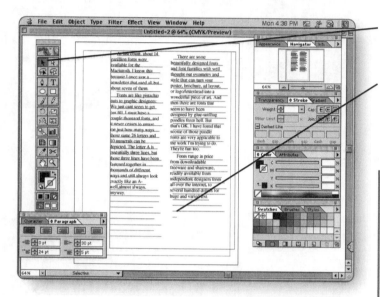

1. **Click** on the **Selection tool**. The tool will become active.

2. **Click and drag** on any of the **bounding box handles**. The text boxes will resize accordingly.

NOTE

Text-linked objects behave similarly to grouped objects—you can't resize or reshape the individual objects without first removing the text link.

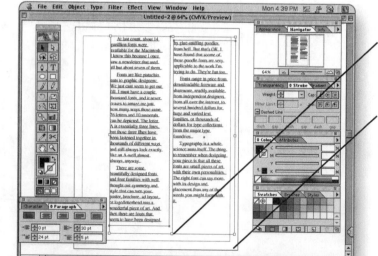

3. **Release** the **mouse button**. The text will flow to fill the text boxes.

4. **Command+click** on an **empty place** on the artboard. The object will be deselected.

Creating Outlines

Okay now, pay attention to this one: for people who want to design their own logos, letterheads, signage, or typefaces, outlining might be the most important command in the Illustrator arsenal. This is the "rabbit up your sleeve" technique, in which you magically change any word, letter, or other text item that you can type onto the artboard into (drum roll, flashpot) an object! Why is this such a big deal? Because once your type becomes an object, you can apply every single tool you've learned to use so far in this book to take a mild-mannered piece of text and transform, fill, stroke, mask, stretch, cut, scale, skew, rotate, blend, mesh, or whatever until you've created the literary artwork of your dreams. There are no limits!

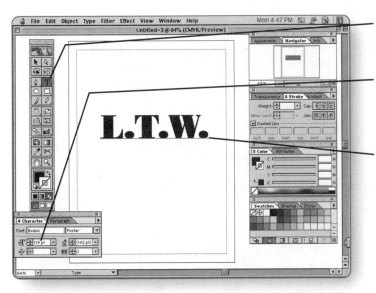

1. Click on the **Text tool**. The tool will become active.

2. Click in the **Font Size text box** and enter a higher point value.

3. Click on the **artboard** and **begin typing**. The type will appear on the board at the desired point size.

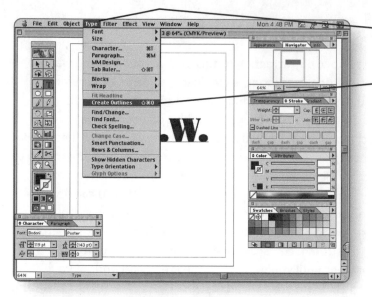

4. Click on **Type**. The Type menu will open.

5. Click on **Create Outlines**. The menu will close and the selected type will become objects.

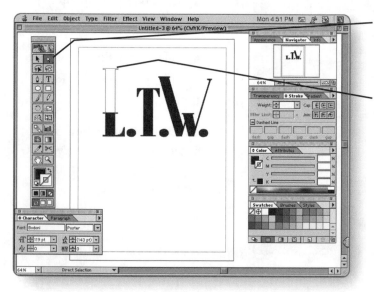

6. Click on the **Direct Selection tool**. The tool will become active.

7. Drag any **handles** or **anchor points** in any direction to reshape the text. The text will be changed.

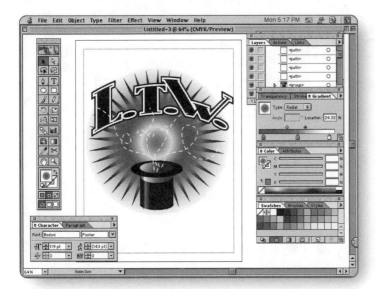

8. Take a **bow**. The audience will be delighted.

Part III Review Questions

1. What type of fill has two or more colors that gradually blend into one another? *See "The Swatches Palette" in Chapter 8*

2. What is the difference between a linear and a radial gradient? *See "Linear versus Radial Gradients" in Chapter 8*

3. Where is the Calligraphy brush tool found? *See "Applying a Calligraphy Stroke" in Chapter 9*

4. Filters and Effects are very similar in Illustrator; which is permanent? *See "Filters, Effects, Appearances, and Styles" in Chapter 10*

5. What does the Stylize filter allow you to do? *See "Using Filters" in Chapter 10*

6. How do you reverse the direction of a compound path? *See "Reversing the Direction of a Path" in Chapter 11*

7. Why is the Illustrator 9 basic mask command called a *clipping mask*? *See "Making a Clipping Mask" in Chapter 12*

8. How does working in multiple layers make complex projects easier and less time-consuming? *See "Digging Through the Layers" in Chapter 13*

9. How do you set or change the color of a layer? *See "Controlling Layer Options" in Chapter 13*

10. What is the difference between the Type tool, Area Type tool, and the Path Type tool? *See "Putting the Text on the Page with the Type Tools" in Chapter 14*

11. Which Illustrator 9 palette allows you to select and change fonts? *See "Selecting a Font" in Chapter 14*

PART IV

Digging Deeper

15

Making Graphs

If you're using Illustrator in a business environment, there probably will come a time when you must come up with some charts and graphs for a presentation. Or maybe you just want to keep track of your monthly jogging miles, or long-distance phone call minutes, or whatever. You can make graphs in other programs, of course, but the beauty of an Illustrator graph is that you can be much more creative with the graph itself. Add pictures, patterns, styles, gradients—whatever it takes to make your graph pop out and get noticed. In this chapter, you will learn how to…

- Create a graph
- Add artwork to the graph
- Customize the graph
- Edit or add graph data

Creating a Bar Graph

The most common type of graph is the vertical column or bar graph. We'll make the graph first and then turn the columns into art.

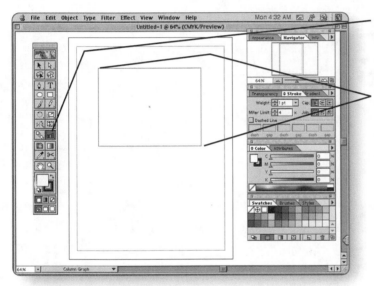

1. Click on the **Column Graph tool**. The tool will become active.

2. **Click and drag diagonally** on the artboard. A rectangle marquee will appear as you drag, defining the size of the graph.

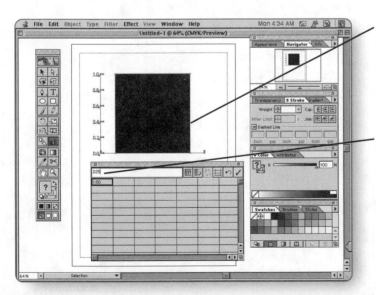

3. **Release** the **mouse button**. A single-column graph will appear on the artboard, and the Graph Data palette will appear.

4. **Enter** a **value** in the Graph Data text box and **press Tab**. The number will be entered in the highlighted column cell, and the next column cell will be highlighted.

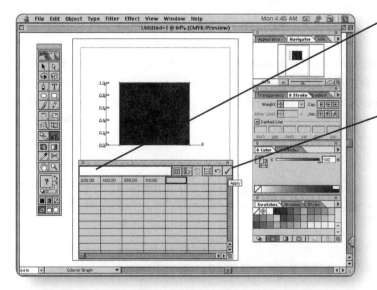

5. Repeat step 4 until you have entered all of the column data. The data will be displayed in the appropriate cells.

6. Click on the **Apply icon** on the far right side of the Graph Data palette. The graph will be divided into the appropriate number of columns, and the column data will be applied to each one.

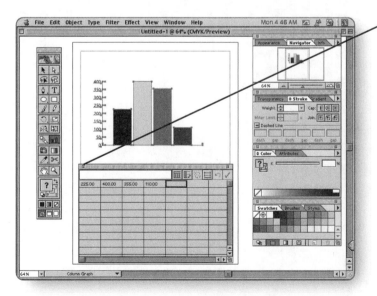

7. Click on the **Graph Data Close box**. The Graph Data palette will close.

Turning the Columns into Art

Here's where Illustrator makes a giant leap forward over other graphing tools. Let's say you want to turn the columns in your graph into depictions of the product they represent. It could be anything from cars to oranges to stacks of dishes to tulip bulbs. I'm using this little chicken. Now draw or place that object on the artboard and select it.

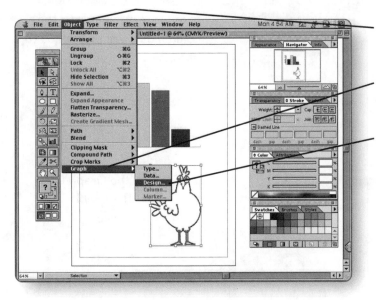

1. **Click** on **Object**. The Object menu will open.

2. **Click** on **Graph**. The Graph submenu will open.

3. **Click** on **Design**. The menus will close, and the Graph Design dialog box will appear.

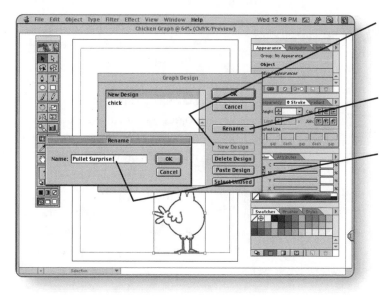

4. Click on **New Design**. A preview of the design will appear in the Preview window.

5. Click on **Rename**. The Rename dialog box will appear.

6. Enter a **name** for the design in the **Name text box**.

7. Click on **OK**. The Rename dialog box will close and the new design name will appear in the Graph Design dialog text box.

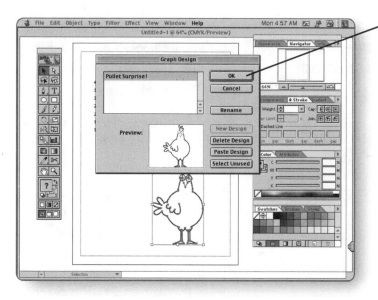

8. Click on **OK** in the Graph Design dialog box. The Graph Design dialog box will close.

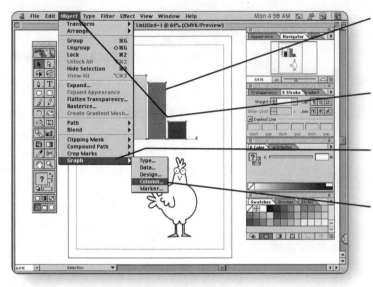

9. Command+click on the **graph**. The graph will be selected.

10. Click on **Object**. The Object menu will open.

11. Click on **Graph**. The Graph submenu will open.

12. Click on **Column**. The menus will close, and the Graph Column dialog box will appear.

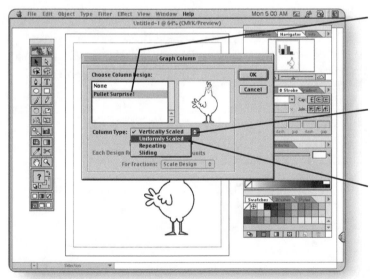

13. Click on a **column design** in the Choose Column Design box. The design name will be highlighted.

14. Click on the **Column Type pop-up menu**. The menu will open.

15. Click on a **column type**. The menu will close and the selected column type will appear on the menu bar.

16. Click on **OK**. The dialog box will close and the artwork will be applied to the graph columns.

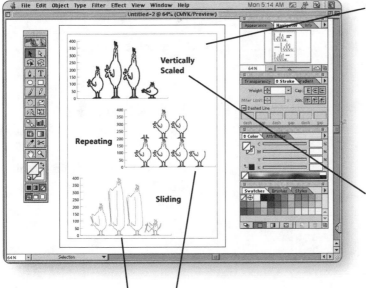

17. **Command+click** on an **empty place** on the artboard. The object will be deselected.

In addition to the Uniformly Scaled option shown in the preceding steps, you also can use the Graph Column dialog box to choose from different column types:

- **Vertically Scaled** columns constrain the artwork to the original column width and stretch the entire object vertically the length of the column.

- **Repeating** columns stack individual depictions of the artwork on top of each other. If you choose the Repeating column type, you must also stipulate how many units each design represents. One chicken picture represents 100 chickens, for example. You can choose Scale Design or Chop Design from the For Fractions pop-up menu to treat fractions of the whole amount.

- **Sliding** columns split the artwork through the middle and stretch or squash it along that line while keeping the upper and lower parts of the art intact.

Customizing the Graph

You can explore more options for graph design in the Graph Type dialog box.

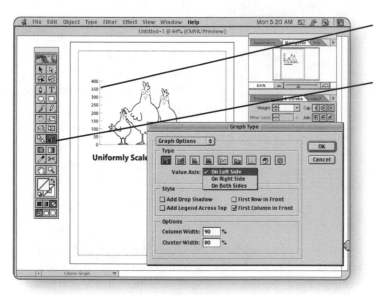

1. **Command-click** on the graph. It will be selected.

2. **Double-click** on the **Graph tool**. The Graph Type dialog box will appear.

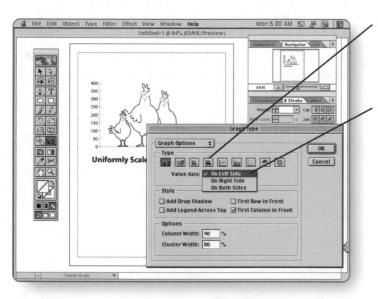

• Clicking on one of the nine **Graph Type boxes** changes the currently selected graph into a new kind of graph.

• The **Value Axis** pop-up menu allows you to list the number values on the left, right, or both sides of the graph.

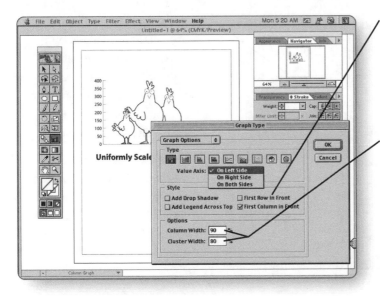

- With the **Style check boxes**, you can alter the look of the graph by adding drop shadows or arranging the stacking order of the columns and rows.

- The **Options text boxes** let you change the widths of column and cluster (total width of all columns).

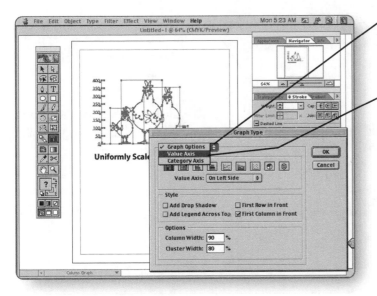

3. Click on the **Graph Options** pop-up menu. The menu will open.

4. Click on **Value Axis**. The value axis options will appear.

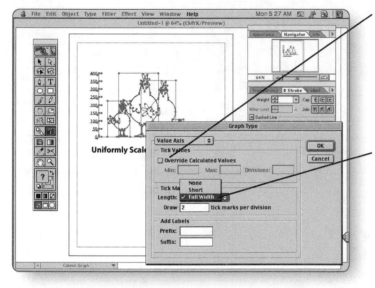

- You can override Illustrator's precalculated values by clicking in the **Override Calculated Values** check box and entering new minimum and maximum number values and a division amount.

- The **Tick Marks pop-up menu** gives you the option of keeping short tick marks, stretching them across the width of the graph, or eliminating them.

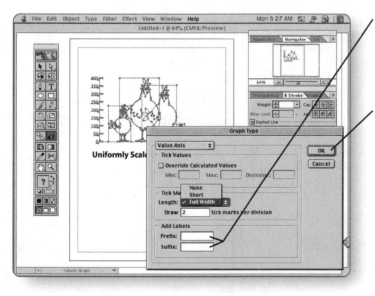

- The **Add Labels text boxes** let you place prefixes and suffixes before and after the number values.

5. Click on **OK**. The dialog box will close and any changes will be applied to the graph.

Changing Graph Data

A graph doesn't really do its job unless it keeps up with changes in the data. Make sure the graph is selected.

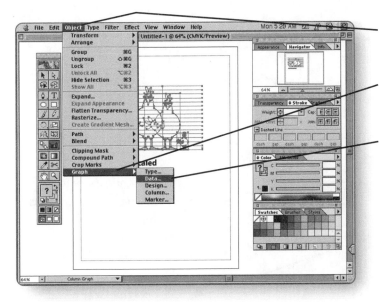

1. Click on **Object**. The Object menu will open.

2. Click on **Graph**. The Graph submenu will open.

3. Click on **Data**. The menus will close, and the Graph Data palette will appear.

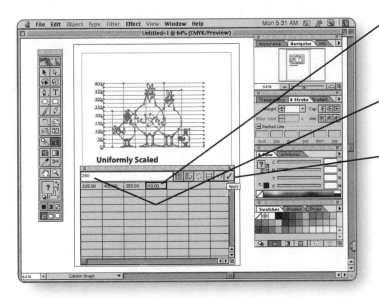

4. Click on a **prevalued column data cell**. It will be highlighted with a black border.

5. Enter a **new number value** in the data text box.

6. Click on the **Apply icon**. The new value will be entered in the highlighted cell, and the corresponding graph column will change accordingly.

Adding New Data

You can also add new data to the graph with the Graph Data palette, which creates new columns.

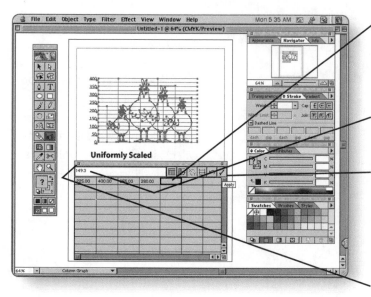

1. **Click** on the adjoining **empty column data cell**. It will become highlighted with a black border.

2. **Enter** a **number** in the value text box.

3. **Click** on the **Apply icon**. The new value will be entered in the highlighted cell, and a new graph column will be created in the graph.

4. **Click** on the **Graph Data Close button**. The Graph Data palette will close.

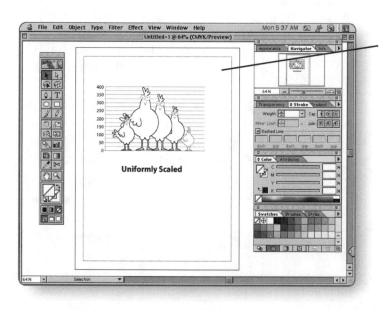

5. **Command+click** on an **empty place** on the artboard. The object will be deselected.

Choosing the Right Graph Style

If you click and hold the mouse button when the cursor is over the toolbox's Graph tool, a pop-up menu appears with a selection of tools to create nine graph and chart styles.

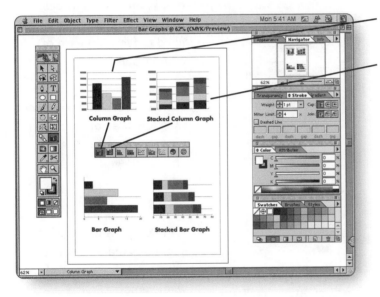

- A **Column** graph creates vertical bar values.

- A **Stacked Column** graph has the same format as the Column graph, except the columns are also layered in front of each other.

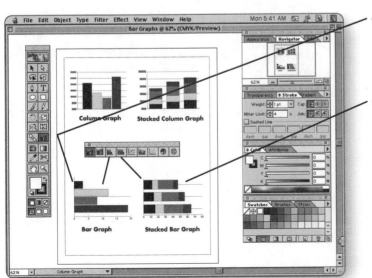

- A **Bar** graph is the same as a Column graph, but the bars are horizontal instead of vertical.

- A **Stacked Bar** graph is the same as a Stacked Column graph, but the bars are horizontal.

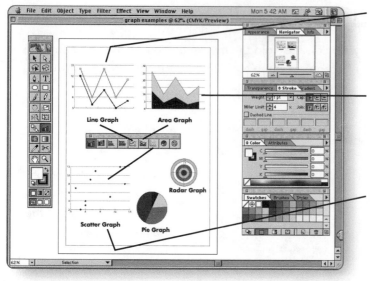

- A **Line** graph measures values plotted along a timeline, with straight lines connecting the value marks.

- An **Area** graph is like a Line graph, but the areas below or between the lines are filled to facilitate ease of comparison.

- A **Scatter** graph is plotted like a Line or Area graph, but the plots are not connected.

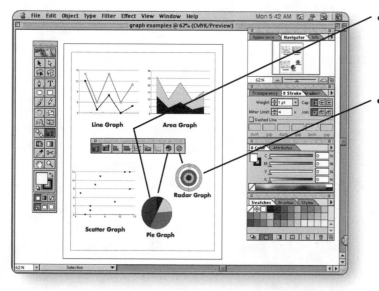

- A **Pie** graph is divided into segments that represent different percentages of the whole amount.

- A **Radar** graph depicts graph data as a circle, with the smaller values in the middle and radiating outward to the larger values.

16

Working with Raster Images

If all you need to create your final project is a vector image created from scratch in Illustrator, you're home free. But a graphic design project more often than not involves a page layout program, a word processor, a Web design application, and scanned images or photographs. Working with a raster program like Photoshop or CorelPAINT! adds capabilities for working with photographs, pixel art, and scanned images, which you then can place, trace, or otherwise enhance. With all that in mind, maybe you can get an idea of where Illustrator's place is in the big picture. In this chapter, you will learn how to…

- Place an imported raster image
- Embed a raster image
- Convert a vector to a raster
- Autotrace a scanned image

Placing an Imported Raster Image

Well, you can hardly work with a raster image unless you have it on the artboard, right? This is how you get it there.

> **NOTE**
>
> Obviously we aren't going to have the same collection of image files to select from. If you don't have a scanner or a pixel-based program like Photoshop to import a raster image from, you can find a bunch of raster images on the Illustrator program CD-ROM. In the Clip Art & Images folder, you'll find folders labeled "Stock Photography 1" and "Stock Photography 2." They are full of digitized photographs in JPEG format that you can place on your artboard.

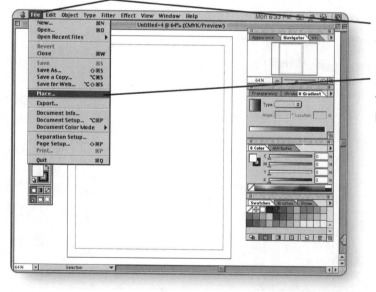

1. Click on **File**. The File menu will open.

2. Click on **Place**. The menu will close and the Place dialog box will appear.

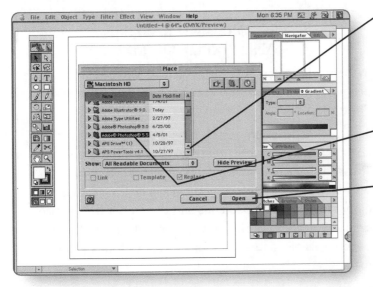

3. Click on the **up** or **down** scroll button on the right of the document window. The folder that holds the image will scroll into view.

4. Click on the **folder**. The folder will be highlighted.

5. Click on **Open**. The contents of the folder will appear in the document window.

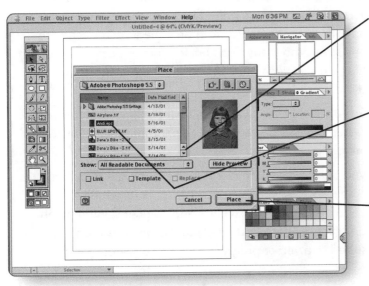

6. Click on the **up** or **down** scroll button on the right side of the document window. The image file will scroll into view.

7. Click on the **file**. The file will be highlighted, and a preview of the image will appear in the preview area.

8. Click on **Place**. The dialog box will close and the image will be placed on the Illustrator artboard.

TIP

If the preview area is not visible, click on the Show Preview button. A thumbnail of the image will appear and the button label will change to Hide Preview.

VECTORS AND RASTERS AND PIXELS, OH MY!

In the world of computer art, you have vector-based programs like Illustrator and raster-based programs like Photoshop.

A *raster* image is composed of several tiny squares of color, much like the dots that make up a photograph. These little squares are called *pixels* (short for *picture element)*. The more pixels you have in an image, the higher its resolution becomes and the bigger the file size gets. If you zoom in on a raster image, the pixels begin to become visible, and the edges of a rasterized object under magnification become jagged.

Instead of pixels, vector art is made up of whole objects that the computer places into particular coordinates. These objects can be edited into any shape and placed anywhere on the board. You can scale a vector image to any size without any loss of resolution or quality. Vector files are also very much smaller than a file with comparable dimensions.

So why would you ever use a raster image? Typically a raster image is better suited to photographic or painterly imaging.

Vector art is usually more at home in the graphic design arena, such as when you need crisp, hard-edged shapes. Logo design, signage, charts and diagrams, information graphics, posters, and typeface design are all very well suited to a vector program such as Illustrator.

Working with Linked and Embedded Images

When you import a new raster file into Illustrator, it automatically becomes a linked file. A linked file isn't really part of the Illustrator document. What you are looking at when you import an image is essentially a lower-resolution preview of that file. The original file still resides on the hard drive or disk or wherever it came from, and Illustrator notes the location of the file and creates a link to that location. The Links palette manages all of the placed raster files and enables you to access the original files for editing.

Opening the Links Palette

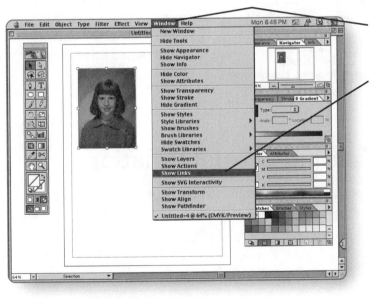

1. **Click** on **Window**. The Window menu will open.

2. **Click** on **Show Links**. The menu will close and the Links palette will come to the front.

Embedding an Image

Embedding an image makes it a part of the Illustrator document. You can embed an image with the help of the Links palette.

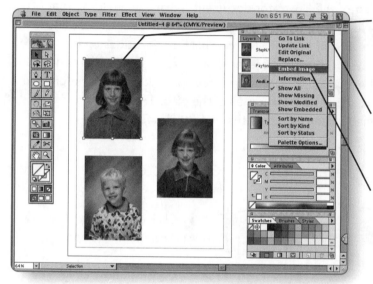

1. **Command-click** on the raster image you want to embed. The image will be selected.

2. **Click** on the **Links palette menu button**. The palette menu will open.

3. **Click** on **Embed Image**. The menu will close and the selected image will become an embedded part of the document.

Getting Link Information

If you need detailed information about a linked image, you can open an information dialog box through the Links palette.

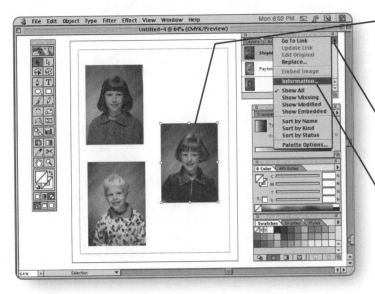

1. **Command+click** on the **placed image** (not an embedded image). The image will be selected.

2. **Click** on the **Links palette menu button**. The palette menu will open.

3. **Click** on **Information**. The menu will close and the Link Information dialog box will appear.

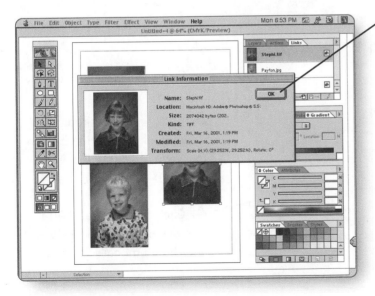

4. Read the information then **click** on **OK**. The Link Information dialog box will close.

TIP

You can also access link information by double-clicking on the title bar of the desired image in the Links palette.

Customizing the Palette

You can change the size of the thumbnails in the Links palette with the Palette Options dialog box.

1. Click on the **Links palette menu button**. The palette menu will open.

2. Click on **Palette Options**. The menu will close and the Palette Options dialog box will appear.

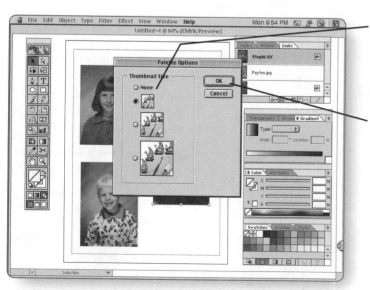

3. Click on the desired **Thumbnail Size option button** (or None, if no thumbnails are desired).

4. Click on **OK**. The Palette Options dialog box will close and the thumbnails will be the size you chose.

The Links Palette Buttons

At the bottom of the Links palette, you'll find four buttons. Their functions, from left to right, follow:

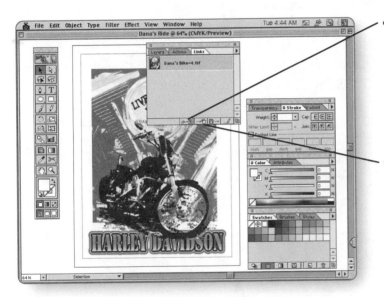

- **Replace Link** lets you replace one linked image with another. The new link is given all of the same attributes and transformations as the one it replaces.

- **Go to Link** selects the image in the document window.

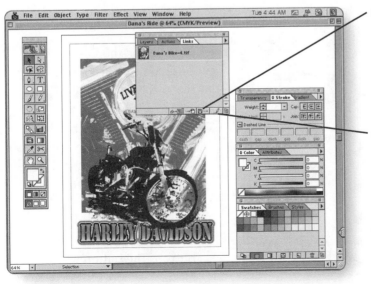

- **Update Link** updates information. If an image file has been changed, an exclamation point icon appears on the right of its thumbnail in the palette.

- **Edit Original** opens the image in the original program where the linked file is located. You then can edit the file in that program and return to Illustrator.

Changing a Vector to a Raster

Sometimes you may want to change a vector image to a raster, like when you're preparing an illustration for a Web site. When a vector is rasterized, it is turned into an embedded image. Create an object and select it.

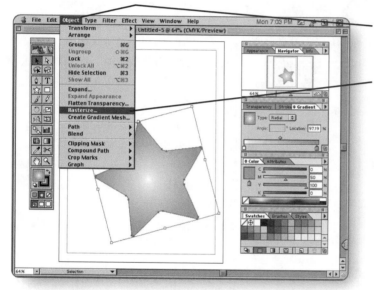

1. **Click** on **Object**. The Object menu will open.

2. **Click** on **Rasterize**. The menu will close and the Rasterize dialog box will appear.

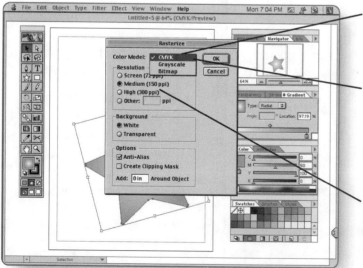

3. **Click** on the **Color Model pop-up menu**. The drop-down menu will open.

4. **Point** to a **color model** (if needed) and **release** the **mouse button**. The color model be selected and the menu will close.

5. **Click** on a **Resolution radio button**. The button will turn black.

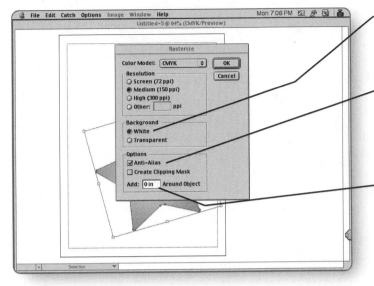

6. Click on a **Background option button**. The button will turn black.

7. Click to **place** a check mark in any Options box (if needed). A check mark will appear in the desired box.

8. Add a **value** to the Add Around Object text box (if you selected the Create Clipping Mask option).

9. Click on **OK**. The dialog box will close and the object will be rasterized.

NOTE

One of the problems with raster art is the appearance of jaggy, saw-blade edges created by the pixels. At higher resolutions, the problem isn't as apparent, but it's still there. *Anti-aliasing* blurs just the edge of a raster image into the background to soften it and give it a smoother look.

17

Designing for the Web

Given its prominence in so many aspects of our daily lives today, it's difficult to remember that the Internet is a relatively new phenomenon. Because Adobe has always been at the forefront of developing technology, it's no surprise to hear that Illustrator has grown and changed to suit the needs of yet another medium, and today's version 9 is completely Internet-friendly. In this chapter, you'll learn how to …

- Create an image using Web-safe colors
- Save pixel images for Web use
- Save vector images for Web use
- Create a PDF file

Using Web-Safe Colors

Because there are so many different makes, models, sizes, and ages of monitors, it's nearly impossible to be sure an image will look exactly as you want it to on every user's monitor. You can drastically reduce your chances for trouble, however, by sticking with a limited number of colors when you design images for the Web. In this exercise, you'll create a new image with Web-safe settings; then later in the chapter, you'll save your image in a format Web browsers understand.

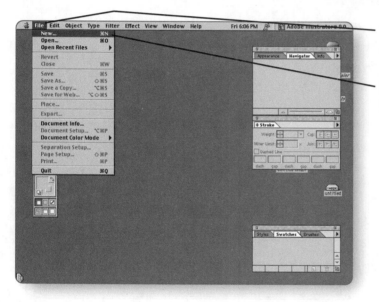

1. Click on File. The File menu will appear.

2. Click on New. The New Document dialog box will open.

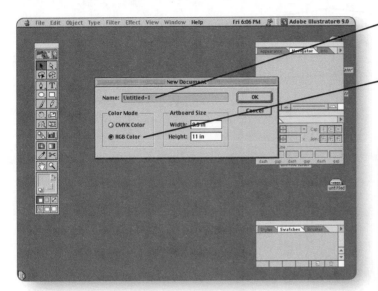

3. Type a **name** for the image in the Name text box.

4. Select the **RGB Color option button** in the Color Mode box.

NOTE

RGB (Red/Green/Blue) mode is the type of color mode your computer monitor uses to display colors. It works by projecting tiny dots, or pixels, of red, green, and blue light in varying mixtures to display up to 256 colors.

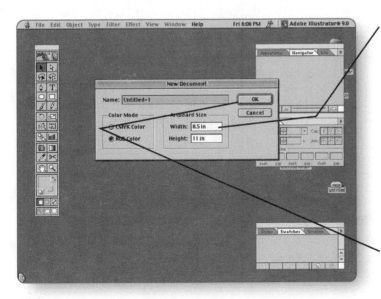

5. Click in the **Width box** and type a value in pixels, such as **100px.** Illustrator will convert your entry to the default unit of measure.

6. Click in the **Height box** and type a value in pixels, such as **100px.** Illustrator will convert your entry to the default unit of measure.

7. Click on **OK.** The New Document dialog box will close and a blank artboard will open with the dimensions you specified.

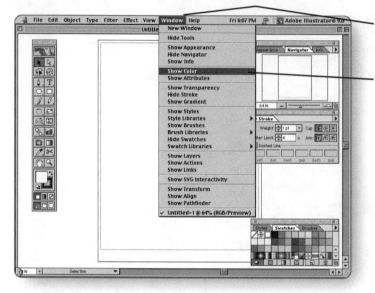

8. Click on **Window**. The Window menu will appear.

9. Click on **Show Color** (if needed). The Color palette will move to the front.

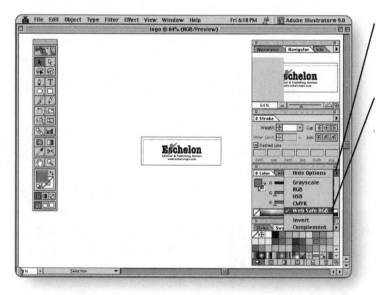

10. Click on the **Color palette menu button**. The Color palette menu will appear.

11. Click on **Web Safe RGB**. Illustrator will reduce the colors available in its various palettes and swatches to include only the 216 colors guaranteed safe for use in Web design.

NOTE

You can use any of the 16.7 million available colors, but the results may be unpredictable. Gradients and patterns can also present problems. Try to stick with the basic Web-safe colors whenever possible.

TIP

You'll find a full library of Web-safe swatches among the default libraries available in Illustrator. See Chapter 9, "Using the Paintbrush," for more details on working with libraries.

You're now ready to create your image. If you want further details on working with Web-safe colors, review the Help coverage on this topic.

Using Web-Friendly File Formats

Although some browsers now support vector graphics, the overwhelming majority of images on the Web are still flat, pixel-based raster graphics. But there's more than one kind—how do you know which type of file to use when? Illustrator's Save for Web feature (an add-in but installed by default) can help you figure that out.

To follow along in this section, you'll need an open illustration. A nice image designed for use on the Web would be great (perhaps the one you created in the preceding section), but you really just need something open onscreen to make the menu selections available for demonstration.

Working in Pixel Preview Mode

The default image view presents a vector-based preview, which might mislead you about the final results by making the image look smoother than it may be when saved as a flat file. Pixel Preview mode will give you a more accurate estimate of how the image will look when saved to a pixel-based format such as JPG or GIF.

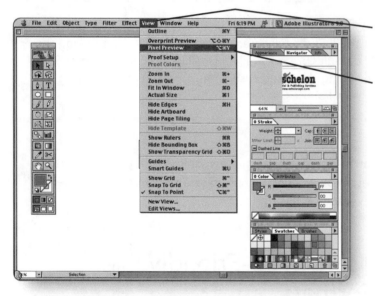

1. Click on **View**. The View menu will open.

2. Click on **Pixel Preview**. Illustrator will display your image in Pixel view.

TIP

Like most items on the View menu, Pixel Preview is an on/off "toggle switch." Repeat steps 1 and 2 to return to the default view.

Saving a Pixel-Based (Raster) Image

If you're designing Web art for the masses (as opposed to those on the cutting edge), you'll want to use a raster image. Nearly all Web browsers can understand these file types and display them without a hitch.

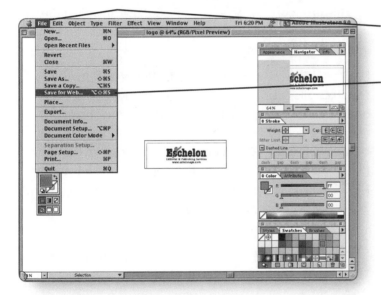

1. Click on **File**. The File menu will open.

2. Click on **Save for Web**. The Save for Web dialog box will appear. A sample of your image will appear in the preview window.

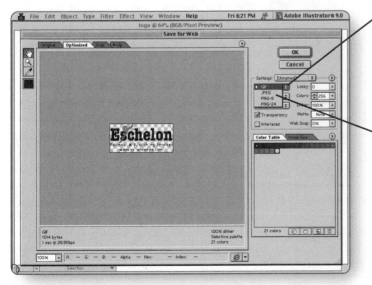

3. Click on the **File Type pop-up menu** (the default is GIF). The menu will appear displaying the available format options.

4. Click on a **file type**. The available options in the dialog box will change depending on which format you choose. The three most common types of Web graphics follow:

TIP

Before you actually publish it, be sure to take your image for a test drive by viewing it in a Web browser. Click the Preview in Browser button at the bottom of the Save for Web dialog box for a quick peek.

- **CompuServe GIF (.GIF).** A GIF file is limited to 256 colors, but it does enable you to create transparent images that let the background of your Web page show through instead of leaving you with a big ugly block of blank space around the edges of the image.

- **JPEG (.JPE or .JPEG).** When number of colors or the size of a file is important, go with a JPEG. You can adjust the amount of compression in a JPEG to reduce file size or improve image quality.

- **PNG (.PNG).** A newer format, PNG (Portable Network Graphics) files also give you the transparent background option, as well as options for controlling dithering and number of colors. Not all browsers support PNG files, so be sure you know your audience if you decide to go with PNG. You'll see two different PNG options: PNG-8 and PNG-24. PNG-8, like GIF, supports up to 256 colors. PNG-24, like JPEG, supports the more robust 16.7 million colors.

5. **Make adjustments** to the available options for the chosen format (as needed). Illustrator will ensure that your image meets these specifications.

6. **Click** on **OK.** The dialog box will close and the image will be saved. Illustrator will add the appropriate file extension (either .JPG or .GIF) to ensure that all computers can correctly interpret the file.

Saving a Vector Image

Only recently have more complex, dimensional vector graphics begun to be integrated into the Web user's experience. Much of this new development is thanks to programs such as Macromedia's Flash, which gives you some pretty amazing Web animation capabilities. As of this writing, you have two vector file formats available in Illustrator: Flash (SWF) and Scalable Vector Graphics (SVG). You don't literally "save" an image to these formats; instead, you export them using a conversion filter.

Exporting to Flash Format

You can create an image in Illustrator and then export it to Flash and make an animation. Alternatively, you can create all the individual "steps" of an animation—either as individual images or as individual layers of one illustration—and export the animation as a Flash file directly. Create the image(s) you want to use and then follow these steps for each necessary file.

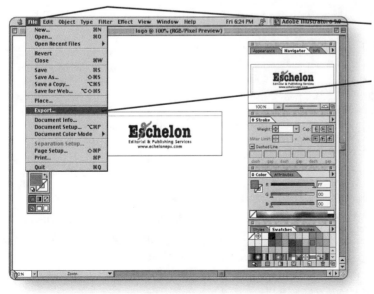

1. Click on **File**. The File menu will open.

2. Click on **Export**. The Export dialog box will appear.

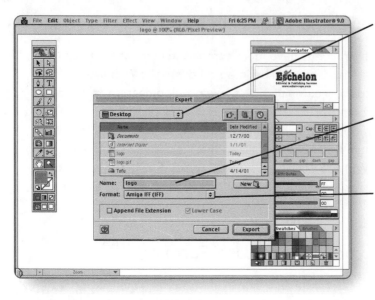

3. Click on the **Location pup-up menu** and **navigate** to the **desired location** on your hard drive or network.

4. Double-click in the **Name box** and **type** a **name** for the file.

5. Click on the **Format pop-up menu**. The menu will appear.

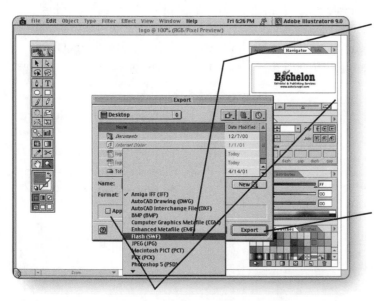

6. Click on **Flash (SWF)**. The file type will be selected.

7. Click in the **Append File Extension check box** to mark it. This adds .swf to the end of the file name (to ensure compatibility with Windows machines).

8. Click on **Export**, then **accept** the **defaults** in the Flash Format Options dialog box that appears. The file will be created. You can open this file in Macromedia Flash or view it in any browser that supports Flash files.

NOTE

You can download a Flash add-on from http://www.adobe.com that will enable you to view these file types with your browser.

Exporting to SVG Format

The Scalable Vector Graphics format is an up-and-comer. It has many advantages over other Web graphics formats, including a small file size and support for embedded fonts. As users and their browsers catch up to current technology, you can expect to see SVG files becoming more and more prevalent in Web graphics pages. Create the image(s) you want to use and follow these steps.

NOTE

You can download an SVG add-on from http://www. adobe.com that will enable you to view these file types in your browser.

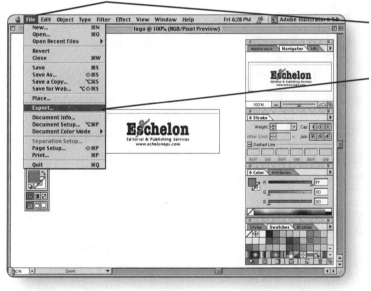

1. Click on **File**. The File menu will open.

2. Click on **Export**. The Export dialog box will appear.

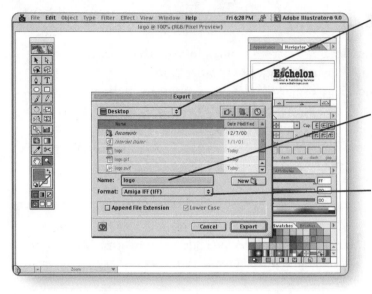

3. Click on the **Location pop-up menu** and **navigate** to the **desired location** on your hard drive or network.

4. Double-click in the **Name box** and **type** a **name** for the file.

5. Click on the **Format pop-up menu**. The menu will appear.

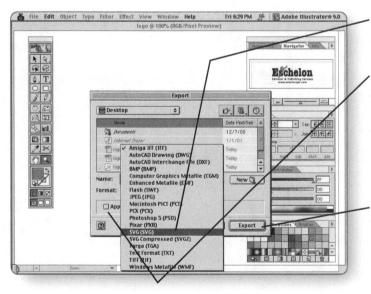

6. Click on **SVG (SVG)**. The file type will be selected.

7. Click in the **Append File Extension check box** to mark it. This adds .svg to the end of the file name (to ensure compatibility with Windows machines).

8. Click on **Export**, then **accept** the **defaults** in the SVG Options dialog box that appears. The file will be created.

Creating a PDF File

Because there are so many different applications and file formats running around out there, it's often difficult for most programs to support every conceivable file format. A "universal language" file viewer is available, however, and anyone can download it (the Adobe Acrobat Reader) for free from adobe.com.

> **NOTE**
>
> You may hear people refer to an Acrobat file as a PDF file, which is derived from the file extension .PDF, which indicates the file type.

If you have the full version of Acrobat on your computer, you can save just about any kind of file to an Acrobat PDF file. With Illustrator 9, you don't even need the full-blown Acrobat program to create an Acrobat file—the format is built in as a save option. You can use an existing Illustrator document for this exercise.

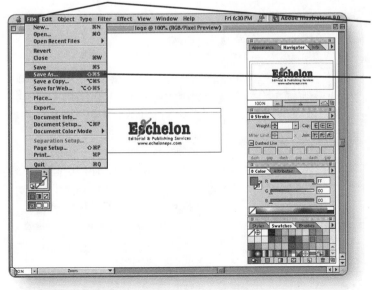

1. Click on **File**. The File menu will open.

2. Click on **Save As**. The Save dialog box will appear.

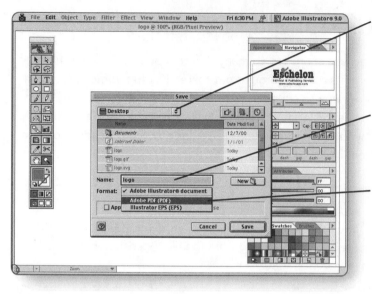

3. Click on the Location pop-up menu and navigate to the desired location on your hard drive or network.

4. Double-click in the Name box and type a name for the file.

5. Click on the Format pop-up menu. The menu will appear.

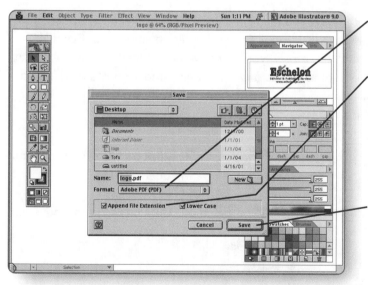

6. Click on Adobe PDF (PDF). The file type will be selected.

7. Click in the Append File Extension check box to mark it. This will add .pdf to the end of the file name (to ensure compatibility with Windows machines).

8. Click on Save, then accept the defaults in the Adobe PDF Format Options dialog box that appears. The file will be created. Any user on any computer platform should be able to view (but not edit) your illustration in PDF format (assuming they have installed the Reader on their computer).

TIP

· You can also edit Acrobat files in Illustrator 9. Open the file, make the desired changes, and resave the file in PDF format

18

Actions in Action

An *action* is a shortcut through the design process that you create for yourself on the Actions palette. Suppose that you could have a video recording of all the repetitive things you do in Illustrator, and instead of having to go through the process of clicking here and there, and opening the same palettes and menus and dialog boxes over and over to accomplish the same task, you could just hit the Play button on the recorder and the process was done automatically. Pipe dream? I think not! Follow along in this chapter, and you'll learn how to …

- Create a new action set
- Record a new action
- Play the action
- Edit the action

Understanding Action Sets

An *action set* might be a description of the place where a *Terminator* movie is filmed, but that's not what we're talking about here. In Illustrator, an action set is a folder in the Actions palette where you can store a whole bunch of actions. For instance, you may have actions that are similar, such as varied degrees of rotation, or maybe actions that just pertain to a particular document or image. Putting actions in their own set is an easy way to keep them organized.

Creating an Action Set

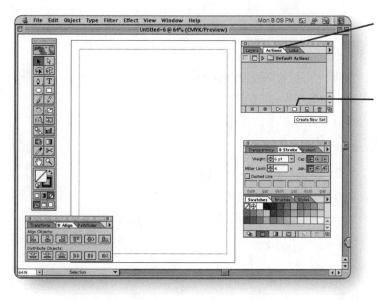

1. **Click** on the **Actions palette tab** (if needed). The Actions palette will move to the front.

2. **Click** on **Create New Set** at the bottom of the palette. The New Set dialog box will appear.

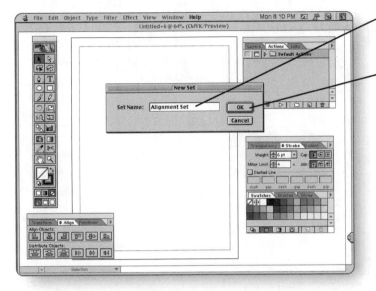

3. Enter a **name** for the set in the Set Name text box.

4. Click on **OK**. The dialog box will close, and the set folder icon will appear in the Actions palette beside the folder's name.

Creating a New Action

So now we'll make a new action to put into our new action set. One simple action I use a lot will select several objects and stack them centered on top of each other. Draw a couple of simple objects to visualize the process. An unfilled square and a circle will do nicely. Deselect both objects.

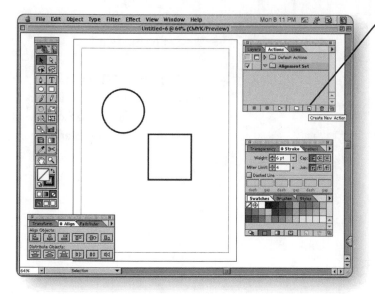

1. Click on **Create New Action** at the bottom of the Actions palette. The New Action dialog box will appear.

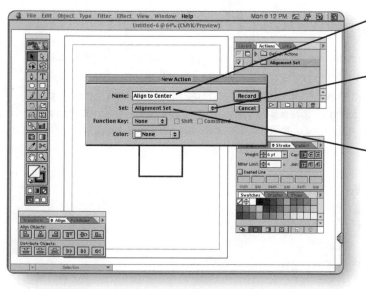

2. Enter a **name** for the action in the Name text box.

3. Click on the **Set pop-up menu** (if needed). The menu will open.

4. Select the **set** to which you want to assign the new action and **release** the **mouse button**. The set will be selected.

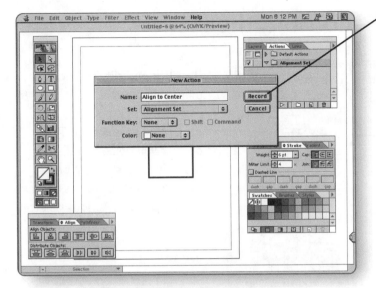

5. Click on Record. The dialog box will close and the new action title will appear below the set title in the Actions palette. The Record button on the bottom of the Actions palette will turn red, and Illustrator will begin recording the action as you apply the sequential steps.

NOTE

You'll notice in the New Action dialog box that two more drop-down menus are available.

• The **Function Key menu** allows you to assign the action to one of the numbered F keys on your keyboard.

• The **Color menu** works when you select Button Mode from the Actions palette option menu. You may then give the buttons a designated color.

Recording the Action

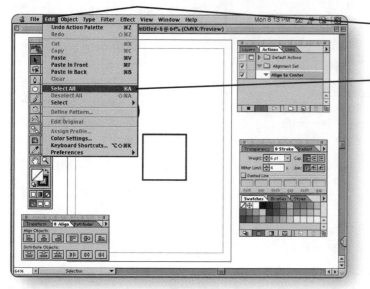

1. Click on **Edit**. The Edit menu will open.

2. Click on **Select All**. The objects will be selected, and the Select All step will be recorded and appear as the first step in the Actions palette.

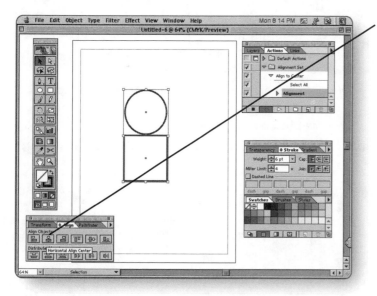

3. Click on **Horizontal Align Center** in the Align palette. The objects will align in one direction, and the alignment step will be recorded in the Actions palette.

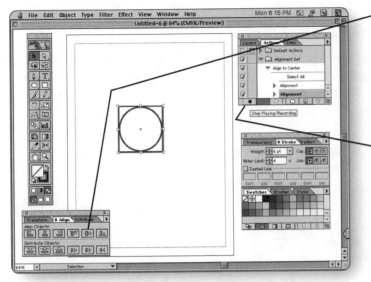

4. Click on **Vertical Align Center** in the Align palette. The objects will align to their centers, and the alignment step will be recorded in the Actions palette.

5. Click on **Stop Playing/Recording** at the bottom of the Actions palette. Illustrator will stop recording the action steps.

Playing the Action

Draw a few more objects on the artboard and deselect them.

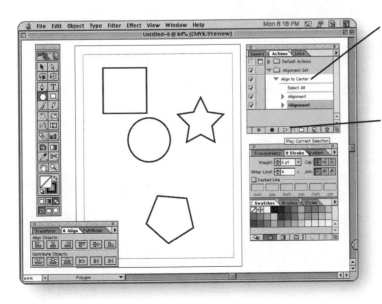

1. Click on the **name** of the new action in the Actions palette. The nameplate will be selected in a gray box.

2. Click on **Play Current Selection** at the bottom of the Actions palette. The action will play through the steps, and the objects will behave accordingly.

Editing an Action

If the action you've created doesn't perform the way you expected it to, you can add or subtract as many steps as you want. Draw another object and don't deselect it. I drew a polygon with six sides.

1. **Click** on the **action name** in the Actions palette. The action will be selected.

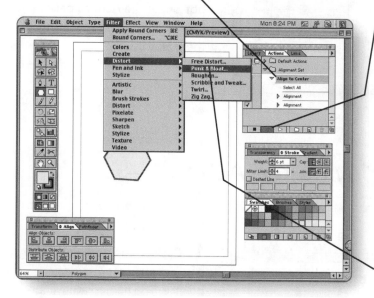

2. **Click** on **Begin Recording** at the bottom of the Actions palette. The button will turn red, and Illustrator will record any new steps into the selected action.

3. **Click** on **Filter**. The Filter menu will open.

4. **Click** on **Distort**. The Distort submenu will appear.

5. **Click** on **Punk & Bloat**. The menus will close, and the Punk & Bloat dialog box will appear.

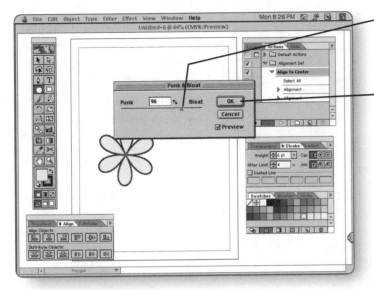

6. Click and drag the slider. The object will distort to the desired percentage.

7. Click on OK. The dialog box will close and Punk & Bloat will appear as a new step in the Actions palette.

NOTE

Use the Preview button to demonstrate the effect before you commit to it, but be sure to deselect Preview if you decide to cancel the dialog box without making the change. Adobe made it work this way on purpose, but it's definitely not the most intuitive part of the Illustrator program.

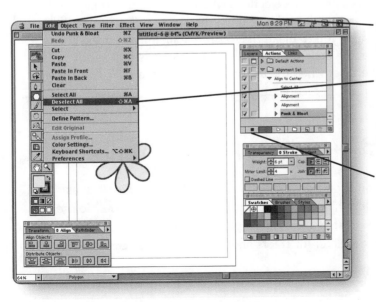

8. Click on Edit. The Edit menu will open.

9. Click on Deselect All. The menu will close and Deselect All will appear as a new step in the actions palette.

10. Click on Stop Playing/Recording in the Actions Palette. Illustrator will stop recording steps to the action.

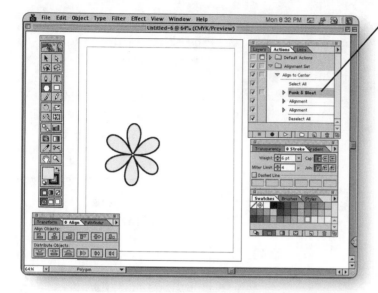

11. Click and drag the **Punk & Bloat title bar** in the Actions palette up to the line between the Select All and the Alignment title bars. The step will be moved to the new location.

NOTE

Notice the two vertical columns on the left side of the Actions palette. The column of check marks allows you to turn an action set, an action, or any part of an action on or off. If you want to run the action we just made without the Punk & Bloat edit, for example, you can just click the Punk & Bloat check mark off, and it will be skipped.

The other column represents those actions where a dialog box is involved. If the dialog box icon is visible in the column, the action will pause, and the dialog box will open for you to make the desired adjustments. If the dialog box icon isn't visible, the action will play through using the dialog box adjustments that were set when the action was first created.

Testing the Edited Action

You should always test an action to make sure it does everything you want it to, and in the right order. To prepare the test, make a bunch of new shapes on the artboard, give them different colors and sizes, and deselect them.

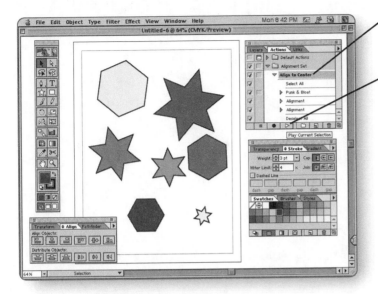

1. Click on the **action title bar**. It will be selected.

2. Click on **Play Current Selection**. The action will play.

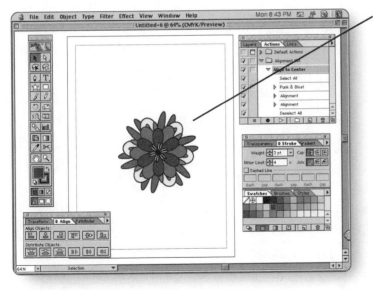

3. Watch in **awe**. You are now awed. How cool are you now?

19

Preparing to Print

OK, you have made all of your beautiful marks on the digital page and your client just can't wait to see what you've done, but he doesn't have a computer or modem or fax machine because he's a Neanderthal. He does have a mailbox, however. So now all we need to do is get your masterpiece off the screen and onto a sheet of paper. I'm assuming you have a sheet of paper and a printer to feed it to. In this chapter, you'll learn how to …

- Select a printer
- Use the Print Dialog box
- Check the page setup
- Work with composites and color separations

Selecting a Printer

I only have one printer on my system, but if you have more than one, you'll have to tell Illustrator which printer you want to use.

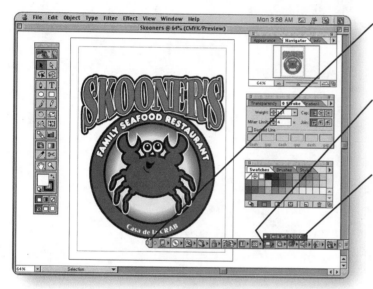

1. Click on the **Control Strip end tab** (if it isn't open). The Control Strip will open.

2. Click on the **printer icon**. A list of all your printers will appear.

3. Click on the appropriate **printer name**. The list will close and the printer you chose will be the targeted printer for the document. (Click on the Control Strip end tab again to close it.)

Down and Dirty Quick Print

If you just want to quickly get the file image on the paper and you have your printer plugged in, warmed up, and ready, follow these steps for a default composite print. Make sure that all of the artwork is in the printable area inside the dotted-line margin on the artboard.

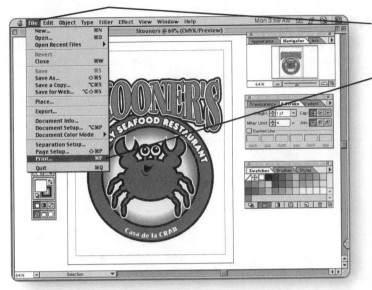

1. Click on **File**. The File menu will open.

2. Click on **Print**. The menu will close and the Print dialog box will appear.

NOTE

Unless you're using the same kind of printer that I have (and I really doubt it, because mine is awfully old), your Print dialog box won't look like this one. You will have most of the same setup choices, however.

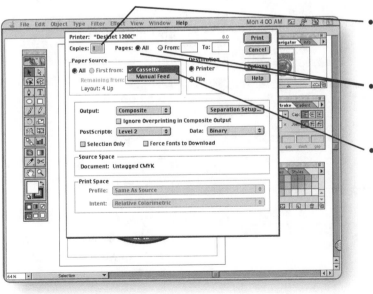

• The **Copies** text box allows you to select the number of copies you want to print.

• **Pages** is for documents that have more than one page to print.

• The **Paper Source** section lets you feed the paper from a cassette tray or manually. Papers such as heavier card stocks sometimes need to be hand-fed into the printer.

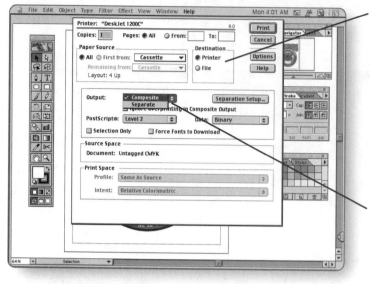

- The **Destination** option buttons direct the document to Printer be printed, or File to be saved. If the File button is selected, the large Print command button becomes a Save button, and when clicked opens a new dialog box asking for file-saving instructions.

- Use the **Output** pop-up menu to print your document as a composite image or have Illustrator break the image down into color separations.

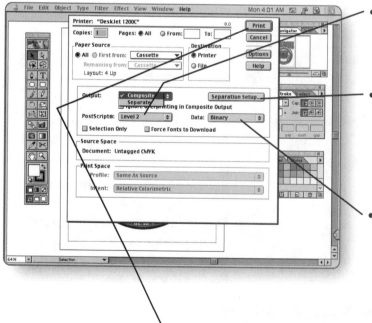

- The **PostScript** pop-up menu allows you to select a PostScript level for your document here.

- The **Separation Setup** button opens the Setup dialog box for color separations. This dialog box is also accessible from the File menu.

- The **Data** pop-up menu allows you to select either Binary or ASCII data encoding. Binary is generally used with Macintosh and ASCII with Windows.

3. Click on **Print**. The dialog box will close and the document will be printed with the default printer settings.

Page Setup

You'll use the Page Setup dialog box to tell the printer the dimensions and orientation of the paper you want to print on. Again, my Setup dialog box probably won't be the same as yours, but the basic options should be similar.

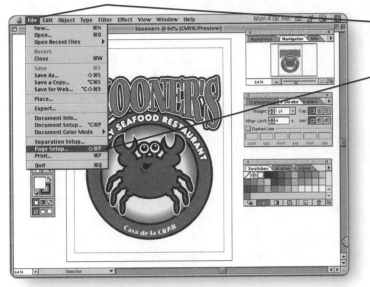

1. Click on **File**. The File menu will open.

2. Click on **Page Setup**. The menu will close and the Page Setup dialog box will appear.

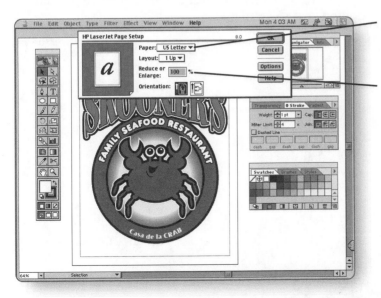

- The **Paper** pop-up menu tells the printer the size of the paper you're feeding.

- **Reduce or Enlarge** (or Scale on some dialog boxes) allows you to scale the document larger or smaller than the original.

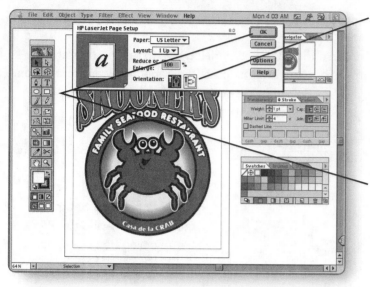

- **Orientation** tells the printer in which direction the image should be printed on the page. Select portrait (with the longest side of the page being vertical) or landscape (short side of the document vertical) orientation.

3. Click on OK. The dialog box will close and the page setup information will be saved.

NOTE

A composite, or composite proof, is simply a full-color example of the image you have on your monitor. If you selected Composite in the Print dialog box and clicked the Print button and everything went well, you should now have a full-color facsimile of the design you created printed on a sheet of paper.

Part IV Review Questions

1. What is the effect produced by using the sliding column type? *See "Turning the Columns into Art" in Chapter 15*

2. How do you make changes to the data in a graph? *See "Changing Graph Data" in Chapter 15*

3. What is the difference between a raster image and a vector image? *See "Placing an Imported Raster Image" in Chapter 16*

4. Name three actions you can perform using the Links palette. *See "Working with Linked and Embedded Images" in Chapter 16*

5. Why would you want to use only Web-safe colors in your project? *See Using Web-Safe Colors" in Chapter 17*

6. What are the three most common types of Web graphics files? *See "Saving a Pixel-Based (Raster) Image" in Chapter 17*

7. How do you save an action to an action set? *See "Creating a New Action" in Chapter 18*

8. What does the column of check marks on the left side of the Actions palette allow you to do? *See "Testing the Edited Action" in Chapter 18*

9. Where do you type in directions to the printer concerning the dimensions and orientation of the paper? *See "Page Setup" in Chapter 19*

10. Why would you want to print a composite proof of your design? *See "Page Setup" in Chapter 19*

PART V

Appendices

A

Installing Adobe Illustrator 9

Just like any other Macintosh application, Adobe Illustrator 9 is easy to install, and is mostly automatic. Just pop in the CD-ROM, provide your registration number, and with a few clicks, you're off and running. An installation wizard does most of the work after you've satisfied its questions. Depending on the speed of your computer, the setup process should only take 15 to 20 minutes.

System Requirements

Illustrator 9 is one of the most amazing and powerful end-user applications ever written (at least in my opinion). While that is a great thing for you, it's a different story for your computer. Before you attempt installation, check to make sure that your computer can support the powerful demands that Illustrator puts on your system. Here's the recommended bare minimum you need to run Illustrator 9:

- PowerPC or faster processor
- Mac OS software version 8.5, 8.6, 9.0
- 64MB of RAM (128MB recommended—you'll be greatly frustrated and disappointed if you have less than that)
- 105MB of available hard-disk space (but you can never have enough disk space)
- Color monitor with 800x600 resolution and 8-bit/256 colors (24-bit, high-resolution display highly recommended)
- Adobe PostScript language printer (if using Adobe PostScript printers, Adobe PostScript Level 2 or later is required)

Installing Adobe Illustrator 9

After you verify your system requirements and locate your product serial number (usually on the back of the CD-ROM), you're ready to get started.

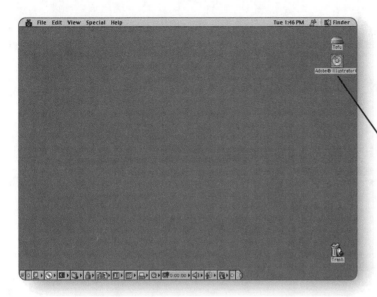

1. Insert the **Illustrator 9 CD-ROM** into your system's CD-ROM drive. The Adobe Illustrator CD-ROM icon will appear on your desktop.

2. Double-click on the **Adobe Illustrator CD-ROM icon**. The Adobe Illustrator folder will open on the desktop.

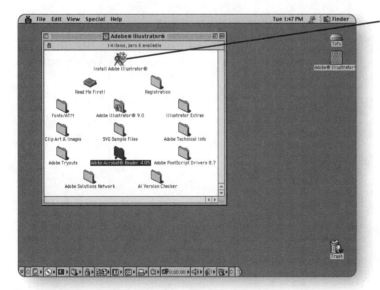

3. Double-click on Install Adobe Illustrator. The installation program will start.

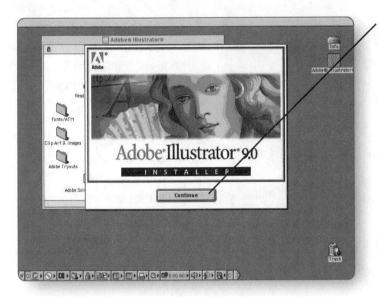

4. Click on **Continue**. The Country dialog box will appear.

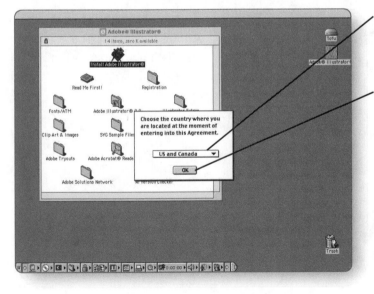

5. Click on a **country name** in the list, if needed. Your country will appear in the dialog box.

6. Click on **OK**. The Adobe End User License Agreement dialog box will appear.

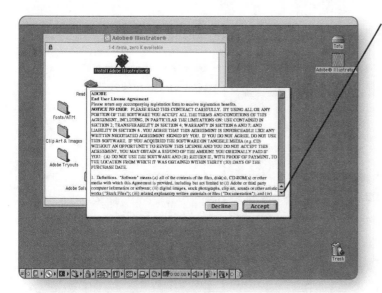

7. Click on the **scroll-down arrow** and read the license agreement.

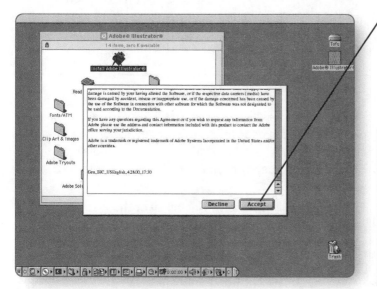

8. Click on **Accept** to acknowledge that you've read and agree to the terms. The Adobe Illustrator 9 Read Me file will open.

NOTE

You must accept the licensing agreement in order to be able to use the software. If you click on Decline, the installation will terminate.

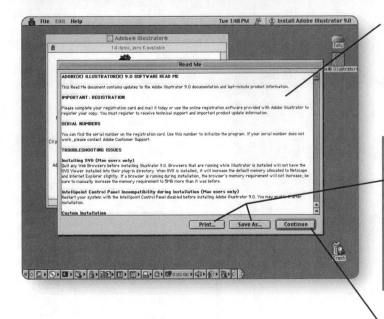

9. **Read** the **file**, scrolling as needed. Be sure to make note of anything in the Read Me file that might affect the installation or use of the program.

TIP

You can click on Print to print a copy of the Read Me file for later reference, or click on Save As to save the file to your hard drive.

10. **Click** on **Continue**. The Adobe Illustrator 9 Setup dialog box will appear.

NOTE

The examples here demonstrate the Easy Install process. You can choose the Custom Install option by clicking on it in the Adobe Illustrator 9 Setup dialog box; you then specify exactly which components you want to install.

The Easy Install process will install all of the files you need to run Illustrator as well as a the provided plug-ins and sample files. It also installs the Help system, which is always a good idea.

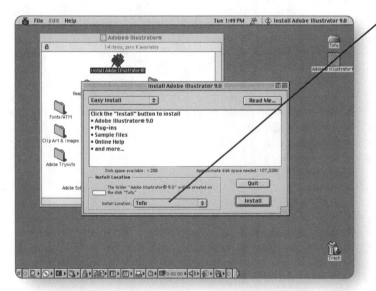

11. Click on the **Installation Location pop-up menu** and click on **Select Folder** (if needed). The Select a Folder dialog box will appear.

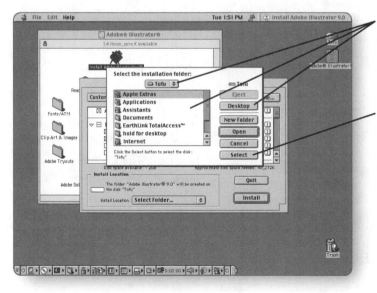

12. **Navigate** the **dialog box** as you would any Macintosh program to indicate where you want to install the program.

13. Click on **Select**. The Select a Folder dialog box will close.

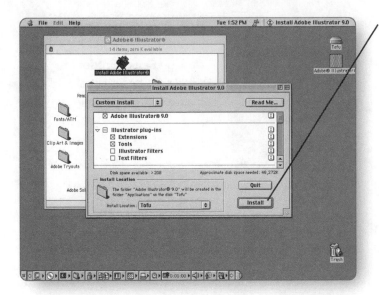

14. **Click** on **Install**. The User Information dialog box will appear.

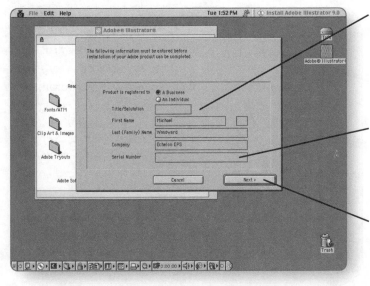

15. **Make** any **changes** to the information Illustrator derived from your system information. The data will be updated in the dialog box.

16. **Type** the **product serial number** in the Serial Number text box. The changes will appear in the text box.

17. **Click** on **Next**. A box will appear prompting you to verify the information you entered.

TIP

If you need to make a correction, click on Back, and then repeat steps 15 to 17.

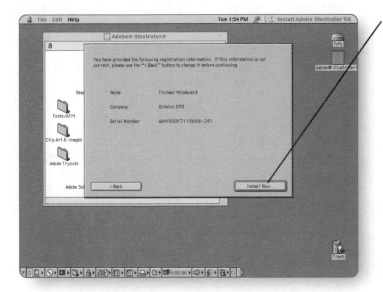

18. Click on **Install Now**. Illustrator will begin copying files to your computer.

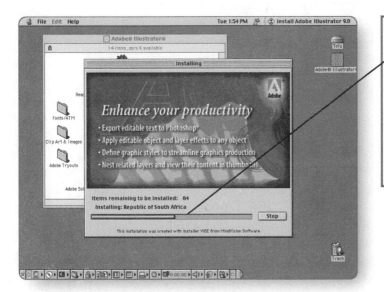

NOTE

The progress bar will let you know how the installation is going. When it's complete, a message box will appear announcing the successful installation.

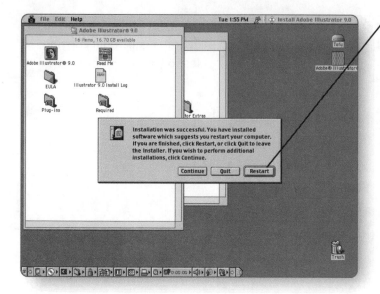

19. Click on **Restart**. The installation program will close and your computer will be restarted.

20. Remove the **Illustrator 9 CD-ROM** from your system's CD-ROM drive. You can begin using Illustrator 9.

B

Keyboard Shortcuts

Because Illustrator is so full of features, you'll probably spend a lot of time switching back and forth among tools, palettes, your drawing, etc. What you might not realize is that Illustrator includes dozens of quick keyboard shortcuts that can help you save time—it's often faster to press a quick-key combination than to push the mouse around and click. With that in mind, Adobe has included many shortcuts, so you can spend less time working with the program itself and more time creating masterpieces.

I highly recommend that you learn and remember as many of these shortcuts as you can. You won't regret it!

File Commands

To Do This	Press This
New Document	Command+N
Open Document	Command+O
Close Document	Command+W
Save	Command+S
Save As	Command+Shift+S
Save a Copy	Command+Option+S
Print	Command+P
Quit Program	Command+Q

Toolbox Selections

To Do This	Press This
Selection Tool	V
Direct Selection	A
Lasso	Y
Direct Lasso	Q
Pen	P
Type	T
Ellipse	L
Rectangle	M
Paintbrush	B
Pencil	N
Rotate	R
Scale	S
Reflect	O

To Do This	Press This
Free Transform	E
Blend	W
Column Graph	J
Gradient Mesh	U
Gradient	G
Eyedropper	I
Paint Bucket	K
Scissors	C
Hand	H
Zoom	Z
Toggle Fill/Stroke	X
Swap Fill/Stroke	Shift+X
Default Fill/Stroke	D

Edit Menu Commands

To Do This	Press This
Undo	Command+Z
Redo	Shift+Command+Z
Cut	Command+X
Copy	Command+C
Paste	Command+V
Paste in Front	Command+F
Paste in Back	Command+B
Select All	Command+A
Deselect All	Shift+Command+A
Preferences	Command+K

Object Menu Commands

To Do This	Press This
Transform Again	Command+D
Bring to Front	Shift+Command+]
Bring Forward	Command+]
Send Backward	Command+[
Send to Back	Shift+Command+[
Group	Command+G
Ungroup	Shift+Command+G
Lock	Command+2
Unlock All	Option+Command+2
Hide Selection	Command+3
Show All	Shift+Command+3
Join	Command+J
Average	Option+Command+J
Make Blend	Option+Command+B
Release Blend	Option+Shift+Command+B
Make Clipping Mask	Command+7
Release Clipping Mask	Option+Command+7
Make Compound Path	Command+8
Release Compound Path	Option+Command+8

Type Menu Commands

To Do This	Press This
Character Palette	Command+T
Paragraph Palette	Command+M
Tab Ruler	Shift+Command+T
Create Outlines	Shift+Command+O

View Menu Commands

To Do This	Press This
Outline/Preview Toggle	Command+Y
Overprint Preview	Option+Shift+Command+Y
Pixel Preview	Option+Command+Y
Zoom In	Command++
Zoom Out	Command+–
Fit in Window	Command+0
Actual Size	Command+1
Show/Hide Edges	Command+H
Show/Hide Rulers	Command+R
Show/Hide Bounding Box	Shift+Command+B
Show/Hide Transparency Grid	Shift+Command+D
Show/Hide Guides	Command+;
Lock/Unlock Guides	Option+Command+;
Make Guides	Command+5
Release Guides	Option+Command+5
Smart Guides	Command+U
Show/Hide Grid	Command+"
Snap to Grid	Shift+Command+"
Snap to Point	Option+Command+"

Additional Resources

This book is meant to introduce you to the most fundamental elements of Illustrator 9. We've opened the toolbox and taken all the elements for a short spin, as it were. But the width and breadth of the creative possibilities of Illustrator and other visual art programs have spawned whole new industries. Hardware makers offer graphics tablets, scanners, portable media drives, and huge flat-screen monitors.

The peripheral software for Illustrator alone is overwhelming. There are all of those plug-ins and filters to look into—and we haven't even mentioned clip art and fonts! Other standalone applications such as Photoshop, Painter, InDesign, Quark Xpress, PageMaker, and DreamWeaver are all perfectly compatible with Illustrator, and using them in conjunction with each other will engender some fantastic stuff.

Bookstores have created entire new sections for the books and magazines dedicated to electronic art and design. And if you have a modem, you have access to thousands of Web pages offering tips, tricks, tutorials, and information.

Hardware and Software

Adobe Systems Inc.
http://www.adobe.com

AGFA
201-440-2500
http://www.agfa.com

Apple Computer
800-767-2775
http://www.apple.com

APS Technologies
800-395-5871
http://www.apstech.com

Corel Corporation
800-772-6735
http://www.corel.com

Dynamic Graphics Inc.
800-255-8800
http://www.dgusa.com

Epson America
800-463-7766
http://www.epson.com

Hewlett Packard
http://www.hp.com

Iomega
http://www.iomega.com

Macromedia
800-989-3762
http://www.macromedia.com

Pantone Inc.
201-935-5500
http://www.pantone.com

Strider Software
906-863-7798
http://www.typestyler.com

Virtual Mirror Corporation
866-386-7328
http://www.virtualmirror.com

WACOM
800-922-9348
http://www.wacom.com

Online Font Suppliers

Every graphic designer I know is a font junkie. Some of these sites are not just for typefaces. They're also informative and entertaining.

http://www.adobe.com
http://www.aerotype.com
http://www.bitstream.com
http://www.comicbookfonts.com
http://www.émigré.com
http://www.eyewire.com
http://www.fontbureau.com
http://www.fontfont.com
http://www.fonthead.com
http://www.houseind.com
http://www.letraset.com
http://www.linotypelibrary.com
http://www.myfonts.com
http://www.philsfonts.com
http://www.precisiontype.com
http://www.typequarry.com

Desktop Publishing and Design Web Sites

The Design & Publishing Center
http://www.graphic-design.com
http://www.desktoppublishing.com
http://www.FORdesigners.com

Will-Harris House Graphic and Web Design
http://www.will-harris.com

Magazines and Periodicals

Computer Arts (British)
Design Graphics (Australian)
Dynamic Graphics Magazine
HOW
Mac Addict
Mac Design
Mac Home Journal
Mac World
Photoshop User
Step by Step Electronic Design
Step by Step Graphics

Books

I'm very much of the opinion that owning a computer doesn't make you an artist or designer any more than owning a guitar makes you B.B. King or Eric Clapton. Just because it is digital and more accessible, you still need to learn and understand the essential principles and techniques of art, design, and illustration. There's a lot of art out there, but not a lot of great artists. You don't need a four-year degree, but you do need to know some basics. These books are a great place to start.

Adobe Illustrator 9.0 Classroom in a Book by Adobe Press; ISBN 0-201-71015-3

Color Harmony 2: A Guide to Creative Color Combinations by Bride M. Whelan. Rockport Publishers Inc.; ISBN 1-56496-401-9

Design Essentials with Adobe Photoshop and Adobe Illustrator by Luanne Seymour Cohen. Adobe Press; ISBN 1-56830-472-2

Idea Index by Jim Krause. North Light Books; ISBN 1-58180-046-0

Illustrator 9 f/x & Design by Sherry London. Coriolis; ISBN 1-57610-750-7

The Illustrator 9 WOW! Book by Sharon Steur, Steven Gordon, and Sandra Alves with Sandee Cohen. Peachpit Press; ISBN 0-201-70453-6

Robin Williams Design Workshop by Robin Williams and JohnTollett. Peachpit Press; ISBN 0-201-70088-3

Visual Literacy: A Conceptual Approach To Graphic Problem Solving by Judith Wilde & Richard Wilde. Watson-Guptil Publications; ISBN 0-8230-5619-8

D
Setting Preferences

Although many people are perfectly happy with the way Illustrator works right out of the box, you might find yourself wishing you could change some of its innate behavior to more closely match the way you work. Well, good news: you can!

Setting preferences in Illustrator only takes a moment. Take some time right now to familiarize yourself with the multitude of options available. Some you'll want to change right away. Others may not mean anything to you now, but you might want to remember for later, after you've gotten the feel for how the program works and how it might work better for you by changing some settings.

Accessing the Preferences Dialog Box

There are so many ways to customize your environment that Adobe decided to group them into specific categories. All of them, however, are accessed from the same big dialog box.

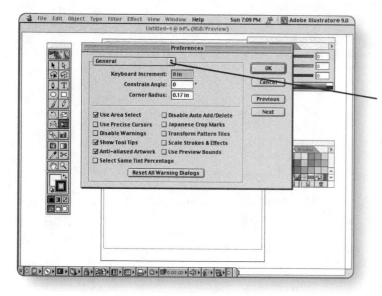

1. **Press Command+K.** The Preferences dialog box will appear.

2. **Click** on the **pop-up menu** at the top of the dialog box. A menu of categories will appear.

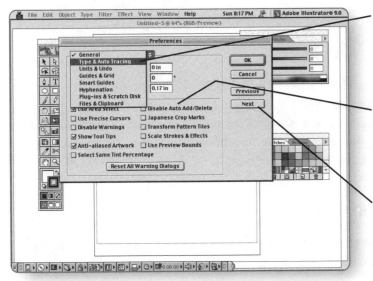

3. Click on the **category** you want to view. The dialog box will change to reveal those settings.

4. Adjust the **settings** as desired by checking or clearing options or entering new values in the appropriate boxes.

5. Click on **Next** or **Previous** to see another group of settings on the drop-down list. The dialog box will change to reveal the next category of settings.

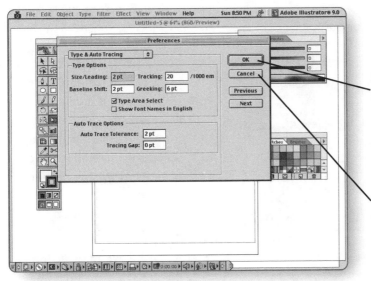

6. Repeat **steps 4 and 5** until you're satisfied with your selections.

7a. Click on **OK**. Illustrator will make the environment changes as instructed.

OR

7b. Click on **Cancel**. The dialog box will close without saving your changes.

Exploring the Available Options

Explaining every possible setting from the popular to the obscure would bore you to tears, but it might be helpful to take a look at some of the preferences you're most likely to appreciate. Use the drop-down list to view the appropriate section of the dialog box.

General

On the General page, you'll find a wide variety of settings, including (but not limited to) the following:

- **Show Tool Tips**. If you tend to forget what all the various tools and screen gadgets do, Tool Tips will give you a hint by popping up a small "bubble" describing the tool's name or purpose.

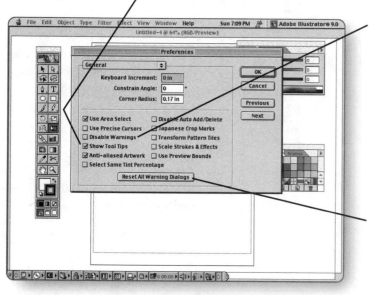

- **Disable Warnings**. I don't really recommend this one, so be cautious if you choose it—it lets you skip the warning messages that pop up when you're about to do something you might regret, like make a change to your drawing that cannot be undone.

- **Reset All Warning Dialogs**. If you have disabled a few warning messages as they appear, but haven't selected the option discussed above, click this button to restore all message.

Units and Undo

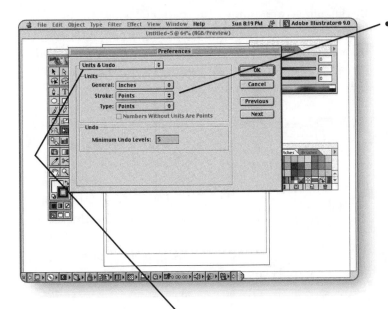

- Change the **Units** settings if you normally work with one particular unit of measure, such as pixels (for Web design) or centimeters (in Europe, perhaps). The really great thing here is that you can use different settings for stroke width, type sizes, and general measurements.

- If you tend to change your mind a lot, you might want to increase the number of sequential **Undo** commands you can perform. The maximum setting is 200 levels—just remember that it takes a lot of memory for your computer to keep track of that many backward steps. I usually stick with about 10 unless I'm doing something really tricky that requires many minutely detailed changes.

Guides and Grids

- By default, **screen guides** are solid blue lines. If your illustration has a lot of blue in it (or if you just don't like blue), it might behoove you to choose another color. You can also make them appear as dots so you don't confuse them for actual lines in your drawing.

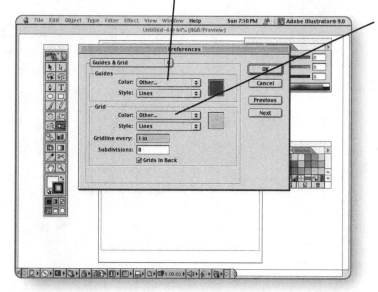

- You can change **Grids lines** to another color and style, too. In addition, you can change the density of the grid lines (great for detail work, especially when Snap To is enabled), and whether the grid lines appear in front of or in back of your illustration.

Glossary

Action. A series of recorded instructions to automate commands that are used repeatedly.

Adobe Online. An online service accessible for information, products, and support.

Alignment. Tools used for adjusting the position of objects relative to each other or relative to the page.

Anchor point. A point along the path that defines either a corner or curve segment.

Anti-aliasing. The blurring of pixels along the edge of a raster image to make it appear less jagged.

Appearances. Collections of fills and strokes that define the look of an object.

Artboard. Illustrator's drawing surface or workspace.

Average command. Averages anchor or endpoint alignment.

Baseline. The line that a letter sits on. Typically, if the type is on a path, the path is on the baseline.

Baseline shift. The distance of the bottom of the text from the baseline.

Blend. A technique of combining shapes and/or colors of objects.

Butt cap. The stroke of the path is flush with the endpoint of the path.

Clipboard. A storage location off of the work area to save work for pasting or placing into another image.

Clipping path. *See Mask.*

CMYK color. Standard four-color process used to create true color in the commercial printing process. Colors includes cyan, magenta, yellow, and black.

Color mode. Different color processes, including CMYK, RGB, grayscale, and others.

Compound path. Two or more separate paths that share the same object to create a hole in the object.

Direction point. The direction points, or handles, are aids to help you draw. They appear as bullet symbols and are always on the top layer.

Distort. To change the shape of an object irregularly.

Distribute. To space objects evenly among themselves or relative to the page.

Effect. Effects are compiled with all the other attributes of the object (fills, strokes, etc.) and can be edited from within the Appearance palette. Unlike filters, effects only change the attributes of an object visually, leaving the integrity of the object intact for later editing.

EPS. *Encapsulated PostScript File.*

Eyedropper. Tool used to "copy and paste" a color or pattern.

Fill. The area inside the boundaries of a path.

Filter. Tools that are primarily used to change the appearance of an object.

Flatten. The process of merging several layers of an object together into one. Typically, this process is not done until individual layers have been edited.

Floating palette. Small toolboxes or windows containing tools and other options to work with an image.

Font. The style of type used to set text on a page or illustration.

GIF. *Graphics Interchange Format.* Can include images with up to 256 colors. GIF formats allow for interlaced, animated, or transparent

Gradient. A graduated blend between two or more colors.

Gradient mesh. A movable net of anchor points on the surface of an object from which you can control several gradients on the same surface.

Grid. A non-printable network of lines to use as guides on the artboard for placing objects and type.

Guide. A line that can be dragged from the rulers on the toolbar and placed on the artboard to work as a guide for object or text placement.

Index link. A help feature that searches an index and links to more in-depth levels of searching.

JPEG. *Joint Photographic Experts Group.* A common format for graphic images on the Web. This format is best suited for images that contain more than 256 colors, gradient fills, and photographs.

Kerning. The spacing between letters in a line of text.

Leading. The space between two lines of type.

Library. A collection of swatches, styles, brushes, or patterns.

Marquee. A selection method in which you click and drag the selection tool over objects or areas of the objects you want to select. A dotted line or marquee appears to mark the area you selected.

Mask. When an object is placed inside a mask, any part of that object outside the shape of the mask is hidden.

Mesh patch. The area inside four mesh points.

Mesh point. Anchor points in diamond shapes that are used to assign colors to gradients in a gradient mesh.

Opacity. *See Transparency.*

Palette. *See Floating palette.*

Path. Any line that defines an object. A path can be open, as a straight line or closed to create any shape. Paths are the basis of all artwork in a vector program.

Pathfinder. A set of filters that work primarily to cut, merge, or blend paths. They are located in the Pathfinder Palette.

Pattern. Any fill or stroke made up of smaller pieces of art that join together to create a design.

PDF. *Portable Document Format.* An Adobe Acrobat format that preserves the content and exact look of the original document.

Pixel. A single dot of color in an image. Higher resolution images have smaller pixels and therefore look more detailed and smooth, and less grainy.

pixel-based image. *See raster image.*

Point. Text measurement also used to measure the weight of a stroke.

Point of origin. A resized object will resize from a point of origin that you designate. If not designated, the point of origin defaults to the center.

Raster image. An image made of pixels. Also referred to as a *bitmap.* These are images composed of individual colored pixels. Paint programs such as Adobe Photoshop typically create raster images. Opposite of *vector.*

Reference points. The nine points of a bounding box that surrounds an object.

Reflect. A mirror image of the original position of the object.

RGB color. Red-green-blue color mode, generally used when creating art for computer images, as in designing a Web page.

Rotate. Turning a selected object to a different position.

Scale. To reduce or enlarge the size of an object.

Segment. The section of a path between two anchor points.

Shear. To slant or skew an object.

Smooth. To remove anchor points along a curved path to simplify and soften a curve.

Stroke. Any printable element defined by a path.

Style. A saved collection of strokes, fills, appearances, and effects that define the look of an object.

SVG. *Scalable Vector Graphics.* A vector image file format compatible with newer browsers. You can export an Illustrator image to SVG format.

Template. A non-printable layer generally used for tracing. Can also mean a sample document.

Text block. An assigned shape designated for text placement.

Tile. A section of a pattern brush.

Tracking. Spacing of a line of text to fit within a text block.

Transform. To make any change to the look of an object—for example, reflecting, rotating, and shearing tools.

Transparency. An effect that makes objects appear translucent in varying degrees.

Trim. One of the Pathfinder filters. It uses the front most object in a stack like a cookie cutter to eliminate everything hidden behind it.

Vector image. Images composed of editable line objects, so the objects themselves can be edited individually and the image can be resized to a great degree without a loss in quality.

Web browser. An application used to view and interact with Web pages. Netscape Navigator and Microsoft Internet Explorer are among the most popular.

Web-safe colors. A selection of 216 Web-safe colors that won't shift when applied or viewed in most Web browsers, regardless of the user's display or monitor settings.

Index

PRIMA TECH's *fast&easy* series

Fast Facts, Easy Access

Offering Mac users extraordinary value at a bargain price, the *fast & easy* series is dedicated to one idea: To help readers accomplish tasks as quickly and easily as possible. The unique visual teaching method combines concise tutorials and hundreds of screen shots to dramatically increase learning speed and retention of the material. With PRIMA TECH's *fast & easy* series, you simply look and learn.

**iMac™ Fast & Easy®
Revised Edition**
0-7615-3136-X U.S. $18.99 • Can. $28.95 • U.K. £13.99

**Adobe® Illustrator® for the Mac®
Fast & Easy®**
0-7615-3502-0 U.S. $18.99 • Can. $28.95 • U.K. £13.99

**Photoshop® 6 for Mac®
Fast & Easy®**
0-7615-3000-2 U.S. $18.99 • Can. $28.95 • U.K. £13.99

**iMovie™ 2
Fast & Easy®**
0-7615-3467-9 U.S. $18.99 • Can. $28.95 • U.K. £13.99

**Mac® OS X
Fast & Easy®**
0-7615-1984-X U.S. $18.99 • Can. $28.95 • U.K. £13.99

PRIMA TECH
A Division of Prima Publishing
www.prima-tech.com

Call now to order
(800)632-8676
ext. 4444

Prima Publishing and Fast & Easy are registered trademarks of Prima Communications, Inc.
All other product and company names are trademarks of their respective companies.